The Art and Science of Putting

Rik DeGunther

A Division of Howard W. Sams & Company
A Bell Atlantic Company

Published by Masters Press
A Division of Howard W. Sams & Company,
A Bell Atlantic Company
2647 Waterfront Pkwy E. Dr, Suite 300,
Indianapolis, IN 46214

96 97 98 99 00 01   10 9 8 7 6 5 4 3 2 1

Library of Congress Cataloging-in-Publication Data

DeGunther, Rik

    The Art and Science of Putting / Rik DeGunther.

       p.   cm.

    ISBN 1-57028-073-8 (paper)

    1. Putting (Golf)   I. Title.

GV979.P8D44   1996   96-11426

796.352'35--dc20   CIP

Table of Contents

The person who enjoys his work as much as he does his hobby is a genius. The golfer who lets frustration destroy the pleasure of the game is a fool.

anonymous

When you miss a shot, never think of what you did wrong. Come up to the next shot thinking of what you must do right. The average expert player hits six, eight or ten real good shots a round. The rest are good misses.

Tommy Armour

Don't try too hard to hole every putt. A 'must make' attitude puts too much pressure on your stroke. Just do your best to get the correct line and speed and roll the ball at the hole on that line.

Ben Crenshaw

Say what you like, long driving is THE fascination of golf.

Henry Longhurst

*I hit short
putts and
stroke the long
ones.*

**Mildred
Zaharias**

Credits:
Cover design: Terry Varvel and Phil Velikan
Inside artwork: Rik DeGunther and Scott Stadler
Proofreaders: Pat Brady and Brian Banschbach

Preface

This book is intended to be used in three ways.

1) The patents, quotations and other sidebar materials are provided so that the book will be suitable for browsing and general entertainment. In this way, the book is intended to be fun and stimulating. Golf should be fun, and so should any book on golf. Many of the quotations are not even referenced to the game of golf, but are philosophical in nature. Hopefully this will provide a basis for some interesting thoughts and insights.

2) A detailed analysis of putting is presented over the course of the book. Hopefully this material has been well written and articulated in such a way that the lay reader, ie the non-technical reader, may clearly understand the technical concepts. The challenge is not in the complexity of the materials, but in the presentation, so that a broad range of readers may understand the formalities.

3) A basic instructional method for putting is presented in chapter nine. It is possible for the reader to skip directly to that chapter and quickly learn a good and simple method.

In general, I wrote this book because I was disappointed in the treatments that I found in other books. Most were simply pep talks given by famous names in the sport, and almost all of these were very dry and unforgiving. Golf should not be work; if it is, it won't last long.

Rik DeGunther, April 1996

If you watch a game, it's fun. It you play it, it's recreation. If you work at it, it's golf.

Bob Hope

The Art and Science of Putting

To Erik James, for helping me finish this book.

Background

Putting and the Game of Golf

Has putting become too important in the game of golf?

If you ask a good putter the answer will likely be no, and if you ask a poor putter the answer will probably be yes. Golf mirrors human nature in many respects. We applaud the things we're good at, and we criticize those that give us trouble. The difference between a good putter and a bad putter is that the good putter enjoys putting. The real question is whether the good putter enjoys putting because he is good at it, or whether he is good because he enjoys putting.

A Brief History of Putting

There is evidence that golf has been played in various forms for over a thousand years, but the game as we know it originated in Scotland before the year 1500. The first official mention of the word "goff" was made by King James II in a statute. He condemned the game for being a complete waste of time. That was almost five hundred years ago, and there are still those who are inclined to agree with him.

The recorded history of golf suggests that the first attempt at setting up a "goff" course did not even include a putting green. A large, leather ball was whacked around the countryside until it came to rest in close proximity to a target area. Very few clubs were used, certainly no putters as we now know them. The rules at the time stated that the ball must be teed up within two club lengths of the hole. Thus, the next hole began where the previous hole ended.

At the beginning of the 17th Century a peace treaty was signed between England and Scotland. This put many weapon makers out of business. To avoid closing, some diverted their talents to the manufacture of golf clubs. As a result, a techno-

Driving's where you make the show; Putting's where you make the dough. This book is dedicated to making dough.

logical leap occurred which vaulted the game into a far more controlled domain.

Golf was played in the United States as early as 1657, but after the War of 1812, disfavor toward anything British forced the game underground. Time heals the worst of wounds, and in 1888 the first modern course was built in Yonkers. The greens were very coarse and rough. They were difficult to maintain and played differently every day of the week.

The evolution of modern putting is mainly attributable to the industrial revolution and the proliferation of machines and chemicals used to treat and condition grass. Evolution in grass types has helped as well. This is in contrast with the fairway game where the quality of equipment has made a greater impact than the quality of grasses. Technology has improved both ends of the game, but in a different way.

Modern greens are so smooth and clean that the early players would probably laugh at our perfection. It was undoubtedly their belief that the random element should play a very influential role in the game. The origin of the term "rub of the green" may be more a philosophical reflection on the game than we want to admit nowadays. Now, a rub of the green is met with a grimace, a disappointment in the failure of modern technology. There is an increasing belief that a golf course should aspire to perfection, rather than character. The two are hardly the same thing, as the courses in England and Scotland attest. The PGA approved courses in this country sometimes look like they were made by a computer.

Putting styles of the most successful golfers in the history of the game have varied considerably. Leo Diegel, a two time PGA winner in the 1920s, putted with his elbows sticking practically straight out, almost a comical appearance. Bobby Locke "hooked" his putts. Jack Nicklaus and Tom Watson both have

If there's one thing certain about putting, it is that it's an individual business. The great putters have used every conceivable type of grip, stance and stroke.

Ben Crenshaw

The Art and Science of Putting

2

open stances. Hubert Green crouches very low over the ball with a very short putter. Billy Casper pokes at the ball with a little jab. Ben Crenshaw, arguably the best putter of all time, uses a smooth sweeping movement, very flowing. And Sam Snead, in his waning years, would hold the putter out in front, one hand a foot above the grass and the other hand a foot or so above that, swinging the putter like a croquet mallet.

Equipment Evolution

The first golf balls were made of coarse, machined wood. These were replaced by balls that were nothing more than leather pouches stuffed with feathers. The pouches were soaked in alum which caused the leather pouch to shrink while the feathers inside expanded, resulting in a highly unpredictable ball. Each ball had its own character, and golfers would have favorite balls which they would use in appropriate situations. Some were better in the wind, some were better in the rain and some were just better. The furthest recorded flight of one of these balls was around 350 yards; however, this record was aided by the wind, which caused the feather weight balls to literally fly. Imagine trying to control one of these balls; modern balls are difficult enough. Imagine trying to putt one, especially on the bumpy, erratic greens of those days. Three-putting was a laudable goal, as opposed to the disappointment it now represents.

Around the year 1880 the material 'gutta percha' accidentally found its way into the manufacturing process of golf balls, and a quantum leap in performance resulted. The balls could be used in rain, which the earlier feather balls could never do.

Around the turn of the century, rubber cored golf balls were invented, and by the 1930's the technology had matured to the

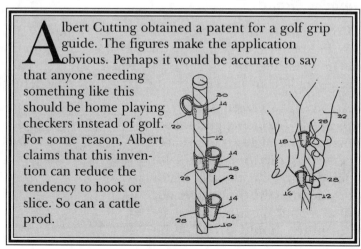

Albert Cutting obtained a patent for a golf grip guide. The figures make the application obvious. Perhaps it would be accurate to say that anyone needing something like this should be home playing checkers instead of golf. For some reason, Albert claims that this invention can reduce the tendency to hook or slice. So can a cattle prod.

Karsten Solheim's first commercial putter was called the Ping Anser. It featured a ringing sound when hit upon the sweet spot. The patent claimed that the sound, in conjunction with the feel, would enhance the effectiveness of the putter.

point where very predictable balls were mass produced. This enabled the sport to be played by more and more people since the cost and complexity were reduced. Modern machinery also reduced the cost of maintenance and the sport of golf became the sport for every man. Dimples, colors, dimple patterns and solid balls soon appeared.

More than 30,000 tons of plastics are used for making golf balls each year, which corresponds to around 500 million balls. This means that over the last ten years there have been over 5 billion golf balls lost. How many of those are you responsible for?

The earliest clubs were made of wood—both shaft and head. As the ball evolved from the soft pouches of feathers, the clubs also had to evolve to meet the demands of striking the new, harder golf balls. Of all the improvements in equipment, the putter stands as the least affected. You could probably give a highly rated golfer on the tour an old wooden shafted, wooden headed putter and he or she could still perform very well, maybe better. This can certainly not be said about any other club.

The technology which has most affected the putting game is the control and development of new grasses, sprinkler systems and mowing machines. Putting surfaces have seen remarkable improvement over the years. It used to be common for greens to be sketchy and rough, and in some parts of the country, sand "greens" were used. On these, you had to take a broom and smooth out the surface between your ball and the hole before putting. A player could cheat by digging a canal to the hole! As we will see in Chapter Four, the quality of a putting surface influences your score much more than you might think.

Numbers Game

Consider the importance of putting. On a par 72 course, the putts should constitute 50% of the shots, by definition of par. On a shorter course, such as a Par 3 (par 54 total), the putting should constitute 67% of the game, again by definition.

According to a recent survey, on a typical par 72 course, putting accounts for around 44% of the shots played (this number should be modified slightly by the fact that a putt made from the fringe does not count as a putt; the actual percentage of putts should probably be

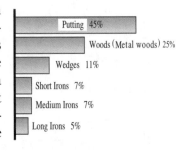

The Londoner who declares golf a moral game is all wrong. Golf is anything but a moral pastime. It is essentially and in all its phases immoral.

St. Louis Republic, 1905

more like 47%). This figure includes all golfers (all handicaps).

The percentage of putts to total score varies with handicap. Statistically, the higher handicappers experience a smaller percentage of their game in putting because it is inherently easier than the full swing, and so the beginner is relatively superior at putting. The result is a curve that looks something like this:

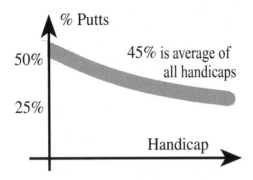

As the golfer gets better, his full swings will improve more rapidly than his putting. This is because there is so much more room for improvement in the fairway game.

A player generally carries fourteen clubs, only one of which is a putter, although nothing in the rules prevents a player from carrying more than one putter. Therefore, one club accounts for around 50% of all shots. Ironically, this one club is probably the least practiced.

Finally, without resort to numbers, consider the impact on score that putting can have. It is almost always true that the winner on Sunday afternoon was putting well for four straight days. Tour pros have very consistent fairway games; the distinguishing characteristic seems to be with putting. A tournament is usually won or lost by a few putts. At least that is the attitude afterward. For the loser, the culprit was a missed three footer on number eight on Thursday. For the winner, the difference was the 14-footer that dropped on number seven on Sunday afternoon. Very seldom is the driver blamed for a loss, and never is a driver given credit for a win, John Daly's PGA Championship notwithstanding.

Teaching Aids and Learning to Putt

There have been, and always will be, a proliferation of golf teaching devices that are introduced to the market each year. Most of these gadgets are directed toward improving the full swing or the chip shot. There are relatively few teaching aids for

Putting shouldn't count in golf. My secretary, who weighs 97 pounds and has never swung a club before, has just as good a chance of dropping a four-footer as I do.

Jack Marty

putting. Given the more defined and restricted nature of the putting stroke, you might think it would be the other way around.

There are relatively few books exclusively dedicated to the art and science of putting. While putting is half the game, it is only around one tenth the market size in terms of books and teaching aids. This is probably a result of the fact that driving is much more impressive than putting. There is no denying it. But a one inch putt counts as much on the scorecard as a 350 yard drive. If you are really interested in lowering your score, the putting game provides the easiest and fastest way. Also, you can practice putting in your living room, which only a fool would do with his driver.

Another reason for the relative lack of concentration in the putting game is the fact that most golfers feel as though putting is a natural motion that you "just do." Stand over the ball and whack it, that's all. This is certainly more true for putting than it is for the full swing. In fact, when most beginners take "golf lessons," they mean the full swing. Golf lessons very rarely occur on the putting surface.

It is true in all of sports that confidence breeds success, which in turn breeds more confidence. "When you're hot, you're hot..." Of course, on the flip side, failure breeds failure. "When you're not, you're not..." The point is that success is a result of confidence. This is why some beginners are so good. They are simply very brash. It's not uncommon for these very same beginners to flounder and falter once they actually start to think about what they are doing. Then the complexities and confusions rear their ugly heads. Welcome to the real world of putting. Welcome to the real world where a sunk putt is the sunshine of a beautiful morning, but mostly the weather is cloudy. Welcome to the real world where golf is the best game to be bad at. And to be good for just one round is worth a soul.

Golf is like tennis. The game doesn't really start until the serve gets in.

Peter Thompson

The Art and Science of Putting

Science and Mysticism

Is Putting an Art or a Science?

Golfers who "feel" their way on the golf course will say that putting is an art. Golfers who "rationalize" every play will claim that putting is a science. The argument is misleading since it suggests that putting must be one or the other. It's actually nothing more than a cultural bias on our part to define art and science as opposite ends of a spectrum.

Putting has elements of both art and science, just like every sport. Certain aspects of putting are strictly technical, while certain aspects are purely intuitive. An understanding of where the lines are drawn will make putting far more simple and enjoyable. A lot of golfers struggle simply because they are using the wrong attitude at the wrong point in the process.

A Notion of Pure Art

Consider the act of painting a picture. While the motivations and emotions that compel the work are intuitive, the composition of the paint, the construction of the paintbrush and the physical interaction between the paint and canvas are all tangible and definable. The painter would be nowhere without the physical elements of his craft. The painter doesn't need to understand physics as a scientist understands the science, with equations and formulas. He does need to understand actions and reactions. He needs to understand how the human eye sees light and how emotion is induced by certain light patterns.

It is very difficult to come up with an art form that exists purely in a vacuum, completely without aid of scientific means. Much of our modern art, particularly music relies heavily on science. Where would the Rolling Stones be without amplifiers and electric guitars?

If science tends to thicken the crust of ice on which we are skating, it is all right. If it tries to find, or professes to have found, the solid ground at the bottom of the water, it is all wrong.

Samuel Butler

7

The Notion of Pure Science

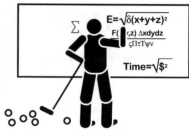

Science relies to a great extent on art, or in the vernacular of science, intuition. While it may seem as if the rigors of scientific methodology do not require intuition, it is intuition that allows science to move ahead into new territory. Science may be learned and mastered, but creativity, "art," is required to stretch the boundaries of what we already know.

There is a huge difference between knowledge and understanding. Someone with a photographic memory can recall every little detail of a printed page, but this recollection is far different from a detailed understanding of what was said on the page.

Science is fact. Art is understanding.

Science and the Essence of Putting

Putting involves physical actions that obey the laws of physics.

As a golf ball rolls on a green, it rotates and reacts to the forces of gravity and friction. These forces are well understood and may be measured and enumerated with a great deal of precision. The impact between club face and golf ball is well understood and predictable. Science is good for an understanding of the patterns of predictability, those things that can be measured and those things that a machine could be programmed to do. We can use science to study the "hard facts."

A perfect putter and a perfect golf ball rolling surface are easy to visualize — as is Astroturf played on by robots. Although we can visualize the perfect putting green with a perfect ball rolling in a nice, smooth curve, we know that "perfect" conditions do not exist. Greens are rough, balls are beat up, the wind blows and our mood is bad because we took a double bogey on the last hole and our boss is overbearing and stubborn.

So where does this leave the usefulness of science, given the fact that life is full of lumps and sandtraps?

1) Establishing Absolute Limitations.

Using science, it is possible to get a feel for how well a perfect putting machine would work under realistically imperfect conditions. However, we can only apply this as a measure of how much we can reasonably expect from ourselves. After all,

The Art and Science of Putting

golf is a game, and it should be fun. Even though it is human nature to want to improve, it is also a part of human nature to demand too much of ourselves. It is important to gain a clear understanding of just how well one can putt; there is a very real limit. It would be foolish to beat oneself over the head for missing a putt that a perfect machine would also miss. In fact, there is a limit to putting which is far short of perfection.

2) Physics of Ball Motion

In the process of reading a green it is imperative to understand exactly how a ball will move as it rolls. The forces that govern the motion of the ball at the moment of impact and until it comes to rest are well known and easy to understand. Forces are the language of movement; so once the forces are known the movement will be too.

3) Equipment

While they have characteristics that can only be described in terms of "feel," putters also have performance characteristics which can be measured and enumerated. For instance, the sweet spot on the putter's head is of critical importance. This may be measured; the size and breadth of the spot can be determined by analyzing the overall weight and weight distribution. And the length of a putter will affect the swing process as well. These things determine which putter feels better than another. Maybe you have the wrong putter and you just don't know it.

A study of golf balls is also instructive. Not all balls are created equal, and there are ways of ensuring that you get good, round, evenly balanced balls.

4) External Effects

Wind, rain and other external effects provide additional forces that influence the movement of the rolling golf ball.

5) Physical Attributes of the Human Body

It is instructive to compare the human body to several very simple putting machines in order to determine how a human should move to optimize the act of stroking a ball.

Art and the Essence of Putting

Once you are standing over the putt, ready to swing, the science class is over. It has to be. The green has to be read, the decision on target line has to be made, the overall conditions must be understood, and they have to be "felt."

The critical process in putting entails the turning of facts and data into an appropriate swing thought, or "swing feel."

Yes, it is a cruel game, one in which the primitive instincts of man are given full play, and the difference between golf and fisticuffs is that in one the pain is of the mind and in the other it is of the body.

Henry Leach

Concentration is intuition, a process of feel. Science is a mechanically rigid structure that can only be used as a tool to find this elusive feel. Science can only open the door, it cannot and will not invite you in.

Fact: Humans can only think of one thing at a time. It would probably be more accurate to say that humans can only think of a maximum of one thing at a time, for it is quite easy to think of nothing at all. It is even easier to think of a confused mess, like a big wad of yarn left on the floor by a kitten. This is what results from trying to be too analytical during the putt process, trying to "concentrate" not by reducing all thoughts into one simple intuitive feel, but by attempting more than one thought simultaneously. The question is, then, what should this one thought be, and how is it obtained?

So putting is truly an art. But putting is also a science.

Jon Cook obtained a patent for a laser golf club putter device that uses a pair of laser beams, one eminating from each end of the putter face. The laser beams come straight from the face so that they point in precisely the same direction as the putter face. This invention has good potential if used properly. The problem is that the laser beams will make a sweep across the ground as the putter is moved, and there is no good way to tell where they are right at the point of impact. And trying to watch where the laser dots are while swinging is distracting. Not only that, but lasers are very difficult to see outdoors, so the invention is really only good in-doors.

The Art and Science of Putting

The Human
Learning Process

Three Parts to Learning

Learning entails studying the gap between intent and result. There are three parts to this process:

1) Understanding intent.
2) Understanding result.
3) Understanding the relationship between the two.

If the intent is wrong, perfect execution will still result in failure. It is important to understand the difference between poor intent and poor execution. Tour golfers make more mistakes in intent than execution. The rest of us strike a nice balance between the two.

Calvin Peete was one of thirteen children raised in an agricultural ghetto in Florida. Inspired by dreams of riches on the PGA tour, he laid a golf manual on an athletic field and studied the pictures and then tried to copy the motions and movements. Though he had a deformed left arm from a childhood accident, his perseverance was legendary and he learned to hit golf balls to a remarkable degree of accuracy. The fact that he was poor and black hardly matters to a golf swing, but it does make Calvin's story more remarkable simply because of the unlikely inspiration.

The conclusion, which everybody already knows, is that learning is 99% desire. If you really want to become a good putter, that in itself is better than books and teachers and clubs and money.

Sports and Games

Sports are played by athletes; however, golf doesn't require that a participant be athletic. You might think of it as a game

An ounce of performance is worth more than a pound of preachment.

Elbert Hubbard

rather than a sport. Athleticism may make learning golf less burdensome, but it won't make for a better golfer. There are too many great golfers that are inept athletes to even allow for an argument on the subject.

Golf is also separated from most sports in that the golfer has so much time between shots to think. Of the time spent on a golf course, only around 2% of the time is spent actually swinging a club and watching the ball in the air. Golf is contemplative and introspective. You don't play golf against any opponent other than yourself. This may go a long way toward explaining why golf is so appealing to so many people.

> Learning can take place outside of awareness (humans communicate a great deal outside of their immediate awareness). For instance, does a transcript of a conversation between two people really contain all the communication between those two people? Of course not.

The brain can learn to associate two previously unconnected things. Pavlov, the Russian physiologist, found that if a bell regularly rings just before meat is given to a dog, the animal associates the sound of the bell with the meat and will soon salivate at the sound alone. A similar process may explain how we acquire certain preferences and dislikes. For example, we can be conditioned to like a particular kind of music because we unconsciously associate it with pleasant experience. Surely this works in golf. If we have a good day on a particular golf course, our confidence in similar situations the next time will be high, and then we will likewise score well again.

The Human Senses

Learning derives from the senses. "Perception" is the term used by teaching researchers to describe the interaction between an event and the student. There are many ways to perceive, some better than others.

Listening to a teacher explain how to putt is probably the least effective use of the senses. Imagine listening to a tape of a putting lecture while you are driving a car. It is doubtful that you will become much better at putting if this is the only instruction you receive. Words have a way of meaning different things to different people.

Seeing, on the other hand, is believing. Watching the pros putt is a good way to learn, although trying to copy them can be

I never played a round when I didn't learn something new about the game.

Ben Hogan

The Art and Science of Putting

ineffective because you cannot watch yourself. You are, therefore, unable to see if you are copying their technique correctly. In this vein, a video machine used during a practice session is probably the best of all worlds. That is, of course, if you know what you want to do. Watching a video of yourself putting may be very confusing if you are unsure of your goals.

The best way to improve putting skill is through the sense of touch, which is called kinesthetic learning. Feeling the weight and balance of a putter can never be duplicated by words or sounds or thought processes. The mind may be set to go, secure in the knowledge, but the nerves and physical movements of the body must come from physical practice.

Compare the putting skill of a golfer who spends three hours a day practicing with that of a well-read golfer who has seldom held a golf-club. The golfer with more practical experience will sink the putts.

> Repetition seems to "wear a groove" into the brain. The current understanding holds that repeated stimulation of brain neurons causes them to grow in both size and number. Over time, of course, the neurons die off without repeated replenishment (forgetting). In this sense, neurons are like muscles which need constant attention to stay in condition. A good putter can quickly become a bad putter without practice.
>
> But beware, repetition of an incorrect movement is learned just as well as repetition of a correct movement. This is why it is so important to do the right thing during practice.

Feedback and Cause and Effect

It was once observed that the population of game birds in a certain part of the country was dwindling. It was also observed that a species of hawk was catching the game birds with a greater percentage of accuracy than ever before.

The effect was clear; a dwindling population. The cause seemed to be clear; too many predators. So the solution adopted by that area was to initiate a campaign against the hawks. They were shot, poisoned and harassed. Lo and behold, the population of game birds began to decline even more quickly.

After a thorough scientific inquiry, it was found that the game birds were suffering from a disease. The hawks, in fact, were catching the weak and sick game birds since they were slower

How people keep correcting us when we are young! There's always some bad habit or other they tell us we ought to get over. Yet most bad habits are tools to help us through life.

Goethe

and easier to catch than the healthy ones. Thus, the hawks were actually slowing the spread of the disease since they were weeding out the carriers. The hawks were actually helping, not hurting the situation.

The point is that the most obvious solution is not always the correct one. Learning is little more than drawing the proper conclusions about why something is not working out, then righting the wrong. Feedback is fundamental to any learning process. Everyone knows what the word feedback means. You try something, watch the results of your attempt, and then adjust accordingly.

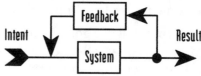

The field of engineering teaches some interesting things about feedback that also apply to the learning process. All feedback systems are prone to oscillation; this is fact. A clock pendulum is perhaps the most basic form of a feedback system. The pendulum bob swings to the right, and gravity pulls it back, but it pulls it back past the center point and the bob ends up too far left. Then gravity pulls it back again, but too far to the right.

This is also true of human nature; we overcompensate just like a pendulum bob. It is in our nature to correct faults to an extreme degree, thereby pushing the fault onto the other side of the error. In putting, we compensate for a slight push by pulling the ball too much. We compensate for overpowering the ball by underpowering the ball. It is always difficult to find the exact, proper correction.

> Practice, practice, practice. What does practice really do? The golf swing is so complicated that it defies articulation. Combine this with the fact that the human mind is only capable of a single thought and the idea of hitting a golf ball seems impossible. Practice reduces the burden on the thought process by making parts of the swing "automatic." The real question is, which parts of the swing should be made automatic?

The Learning Curve

It is easier to go from a 30 handicap to a 20 than it is to go from a 10 handicap to a zero. Each leap in improvement shaves

The Art and Science of Putting

ten strokes, but there is a world of difference. The learning curve describes this phenomenon.

In business the learning curve is used to describe how an organization becomes more efficient as it practices a skill more and more. For instance, a manufacturer will see unit cost reduction as volume increases.

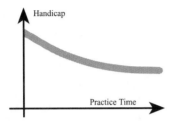

As the volume of production increases, the unit cost decreases. The learning curve applies in golf as well.

As you increase your practice time, your handicap will go down, but your improvement will eventually level out. You need to practice much harder to see improvement when you are a good player than when you are just beginning. For the best pros, constant practice only means maintenance; they do not really get much better, but they have to keep working very hard just to stay on the same level. What does this say about human endeavor?

The point should be obvious; you can only get out of the game what you put into it. If you practice every day, you may reasonably expect to get your handicap down to around five or less. However, if you practice once every two weeks, you should expect far less. When you start to expect more from yourself than is fair or reasonable, then you stop having fun.

The Physics of a Rolling Golf Ball

4

Isaac Newton and the Obvious Apple

The foundation of a building is based on the laws of engineering and science. Above all else, you want the foundation to do its job, to perform its function. You need to trust it and know it will never move. Later, when the frame and the structure are finished, you work on the colors and the "feel" and the personality.

The same is true with a putting stroke. You begin with the fundamentals, the inescapable factors that hold true for every golfer.

The next several chapters present a technical foundation that may at first seem rather intuitive and obvious, but consider this: Isaac Newton was sitting under a tree when an apple fell on his head. According to the story, this resulted in the theory of gravity.

Of course, everybody knew that an apple falls. But an intuitive observation is quite different from an in-depth understanding. While it had always been obvious that an apple falls to the ground, it was not until Newton devised his mathematical description that a true understanding was possible. And by the process of scientifically describing what everyone already knew, and could already see, a whole new world of unseen experience arose.

In fact, as a result of Newton's theory, some things that seemed intuitively obvious were shown to be untrue. For instance, the laws of physics say that a feather and a bowling ball dropped from the same height will fall under the influence of gravity at the same rate. Therefore, they will hit the ground at the same time. Of course this is not our observation since the effect of air resistance severely hinders the feather while causing little problem for the bowling ball. We incorrectly conclude that gravity pulls faster on the bowling ball than the feather. If

Golf is a game in which you yell fore, shoot six, and write down five.

Paul Harvey

17

we only have observation to base our conclusions on, we would have to say that the bowling ball falls faster.

Ideal Putting

To learn how to putt, we must first understand the process of putting. We begin the analysis with a flawless green and a flawless, round golf ball. We eliminate the putter and simply start the ball rolling at a perfectly controlled speed, in a perfectly controlled direction. We want to focus on the most basic physics, so we eliminate all imperfections such as lumps in the grass.

We could, if we wanted, build a device that would approximate these perfect conditions. We could put some very smooth, even carpet onto a rigid plywood panel, and then put a hinge onto the edge of the plywood panel so it could be tilted and moved around.

To get the ball rolling, we could use a simple ramp arrangement.

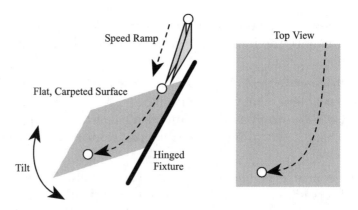

We could make our system work so well that when we repeat an experiment one hundred times in a row, the ball will roll over the same curve each time. Depending on how much time and money we spent building the system, it could be made as accurate as we wanted.

Computer Modeling

To make life easier, I devised a computer model for a rolling golf ball. The output shows a curve of the roll path, exactly like the right-hand side of the above figure.

Now the model can analyze imperfections from such things as lumps in the grass, bad golf balls and human error. The friction may be varied, which corresponds to varying the length of grass. Wind and any combination of weather and conditions can be added.

All these things could be done with the plywood panel and ramp, but it is much easier to isolate the various effects with a computer model. In real life it is difficult to set up an experiment that eliminates all sources of error but the one that we want to study. We only want to look at one kind of error at a time, otherwise we won't be able to draw accurate conclusions concerning cause and effect. The following figure shows an output from the computer model for the perfect conditions described before:

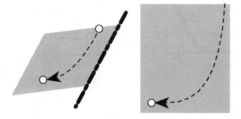

The green is perfectly flat, but tilted, as shown. An amount of friction is applied between the ball and the green, simulating the effect of grass. We need some friction or the ball would simply roll down the hill with increasing speed, like a ball bearing on the hood of a car.

Giving a mathematical name to the curves, or trying to describe them in words does no good. You simply have to look at the "shape" and when you are standing on a green trying to determine the line of your putt, you need to approximate the curve in your mind.

It's not that difficult to do, and you do not have to be a mathematician to do an adequate job.

Most golfers tend to picture an evenly curving trajectory, more like a portion of a circle than the real thing.

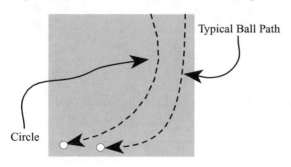

Typical Ball Path

Circle

The Physics of a Rolling Golf Ball

When putting sense and inspiration desert me, I resort to putting by aid of mechanical theory.

Seymour Dunn

Note that at the beginning of the real trajectory there is very little curvature; most is at the end. Compare this with the portion of a circle where the curvature is constant.

Tilting the Green Side to Side

First we will vary the tilt of the green from side to side and see what happens to the curves.

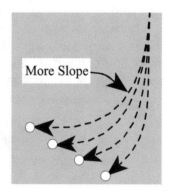

As the side slope increases, the ball begins to curve earlier (a poor word to use, but you catch the drift), but the overall "shape" of the curves are basically the same.

Forward Tilt

Next we can tilt the green forward and backward (keeping the sideward tilt constant).

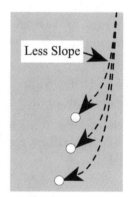

Varying Friction

Here is what happens when the friction of the green is varied, which corresponds to longer or shorter grass.

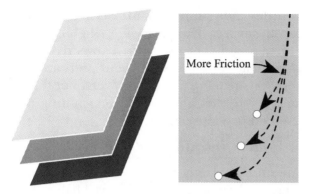

Compare the results of longer grass with an uphill slope and see that the two are different. The force of friction always impedes the forward motion of the ball while a slope induces a force that always points in a constant direction, independent of the direction the ball is moving.

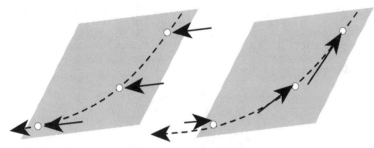

Gravitational force Due to Slope   Friction Forces Always Impede Motion

Varying Speed and Direction

All the experiments so far have been with a constant initial speed and direction. We want to take a look at what happens if we vary the starting conditions, namely initial speed and initial direction.

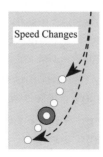 

The Physics of a Rolling Golf Ball

Error in direction and error in speed create far different effects, as you can see. Humans will err in both speed and direction, with most golfers tending more toward one or the other. If you pay more attention to where your putts are missing, you will find that you are more prone to one error or the other. This can be done if you keep a record of your putting (a way to do this is presented in a later chapter).

Different Routes Into the Hole

It is interesting to study how many different ways (combinations of speed and direction) we can start a ball rolling and still have it end up in the cup. We can place an imaginary hole at a spot on our computerized green, and whenever a ball rolls over the hole we will say that it has gone into the hole. We can even make this more realistic by assigning a maximum speed at the hole since we know that the ball will simply jump over the hole if it's going too fast.

There are always a series of curves that will result in the ball passing over the hole. Each of these curves has a different initial speed and direction:

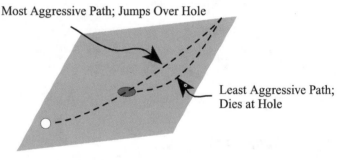

Most Aggressive Path; Jumps Over Hole

Least Aggressive Path; Dies at Hole

This illustrates a flaw in reasoning that most golfers commit when they are lining up a putt; they see one path to the hole, not a range of choices. But there are always a number of trajectories to the hole. There is an aggressive path, which will leave the ball dangerously past the hole if the putt is missed, and there is a conservative path where the ball just barely makes it to the hole. A little less speed than the conservative path demands results in a short putt. Never up, never in.

If you are aggressive, you must undercompensate for slope and the opposite holds true if you are conservative.

The range of possibilities depends on the situation. Uphill putts leave more room for error and downhill putts leave less room for error.

The Art and Science of Putting

Wind

For the sake of this experiment, we will assume that wind blows in a constant direction and has the same effect on the motion as slope, since the direction and magnitude of the force is constant.

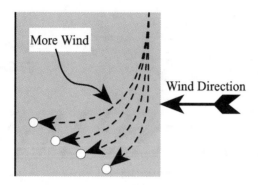

So wind can be viewed as nothing more than a change in the effective slope. Measure where the wind comes from and add or subtract slope to the green accordingly. I have met very few golfers who allow for wind, even though it is a very real influence and easy to compensate for. Deciding how *much* to compensate is the problem, not deciding how to compensate.

Impossible Putts

It is interesting to see if there are conditions under which a putt simply cannot be made. Of course there will always be some trajectory which will ensure that the ball goes over the hole. The real question is one of speed. A ball traveling fast enough will simply jump over the hole and not fall into the cup.

Just as we would expect, the model tells us that on some downhill putts there are conditions where the ball simply will not slow down enough to go into the hole. Any initial rolling at all will increase in speed. This will result from very fast greens or slopes that are too steep to be practical.

If a putt is uphill, there is no possibility of an impossibility, although the putt may be extremely tricky. Uphill putts always leave more room for error, and it is a wise golfer that remembers this when analyzing and planning approach shots and chip shots. Most golfers shoot at the pin itself, which should result in an even spread of shots around the pin, leaving as many downhill putts as uphill ones.

Facts do not cease to exist because they are ignored.

Aldous Huxley

Effects of Grass Grain

Grass hardly ever grows straight upward. Its direction is influenced by drainage and by Mother Nature and all her unexplainable vagaries. Here is what happens due to grass grain.

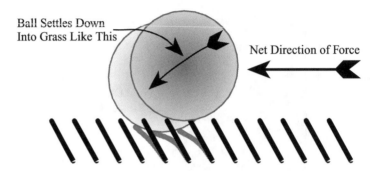

Ball Settles Down Into Grass Like This

Net Direction of Force

The net result is a force that pushes the ball in the direction that the grass is pointing, which should be easy to remember. It's much more difficult to estimate the magnitude of the force than the direction. This will depend on the stiffness of the grass more than anything else, but there is no way to actually estimate it by anything other than intuition trained by experience.

Wet Grass

This is the same as adding friction, or grass length. Early morning greens often have a coating of dew. You need to kick up the initial speed.

Compound Curvatures

Obviously real greens are not nice flat surfaces like we have been using. We could use compound curvatures in the computer, but this really adds nothing to our understanding for two reasons. First, it is impossible to draw such a surface on a sheet of paper, so it would be impossible to demonstrate anything worthwhile within the pages of a book. Second, any such slope can be viewed as a series of small, flat surfaces.

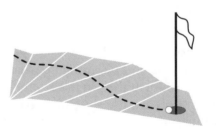

No amount of eccentric implements will make a bad putter putt better.

WT Linskill

The Art and Science of Putting

Real Conditions

Human Touch—Randomness

We will still use the perfect green, ball and roll, but now we add some randomness to the initial speed and direction.

Here is what happens when we allow random errors in both speed and direction.

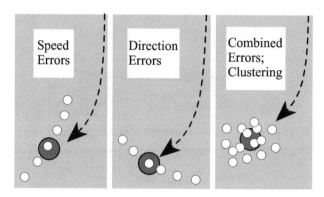

If we vary the mix of errors we get "clustering," which looks like a dartboard full of darts. Here are the relative clusters for two players, a 12 handicap and a 24 handicap.

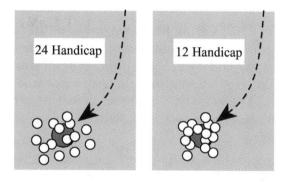

It is easy to see which putts would have gone into the hole.

Lumpy Golf Balls

Real golf balls are not perfect spheres. You can easily see this with Balata balls when they are pushed out of shape. They become squashed out, almost like an egg.

In fact, most golf balls are subject to flaws. The most common flaw is when the center of gravity does not match the physical center of the ball. This is equivalent to a tire being out of balance; the result is a wobble. When it happens on your car, you can feel it and you can then get it fixed. Unfortunately, in

The only certainty is that nothing is certain.

Pliny the Elder

golf you do not feel the problem, although the ball may wobble and act as erratically as an unbalanced tire. You can make an easy measurement to determine the quality of a golf ball. Pour some Epsom salt (easy to get in a drug store) into a glass of water and add a little cooking oil. If you pour in enough Epsom salt, the golf ball will eventually float. Now if the center of gravity is not located at the center of the ball, the ball will settle and turn in the water until one spot is at the top, as shown.

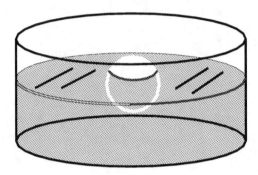

Regardless of where you start the ball, this particular spot will always migrate to the top, near the surface of the liquid. If you wait until the ball settles and make a mark at the topmost spot, then repeat the experiment, the same spot will rise to the top.

A good golf ball will not have a preferred position as it floats. It will just sit in the water, uncaring. Set a good golf ball spinning in the water and it will keep spinning on the same axis and eventually slow down and stop without turning around and adjusting itself. The same type of physics is true for a rolling ball, and it should be clear that an unbalanced, rolling golf ball will not roll perfectly straight.

According to the manufacturers, most golf balls are fine, at least when they are brand new. But the violence of being struck tends to make balls become lopsided. Obviously this is more of a problem for the heavy hitters. It is also more or less of a problem for different manufacturers. It would be useless to try to present a generalization here since manufacturing tolerances vary not only between brands, but over time in a given brand as well. Using high quality, new balls is the best bet.

We can use our same computer program to generate results for bad golf balls.

We will use the perfect green and the perfect initial roll, with perfect direction and speed. We are interested only in how the golf ball imperfection affects the path.

Holing pressure putts isn't a matter of inherited talent or divine inspiration.

George Archer

The Art and Science of Putting

The effect is to cause a cluster much like human randomness. However, note that the cluster is shorter of the hole. This is because wobble steals momentum.

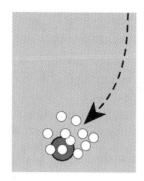

The error from a bad ball manifests itself over the entire roll path. The error from human randomness only occurs at the initial impact. This hardly matters to the end result, however.

Lumpy Greens

So far we have used only perfect greens. We now need to look at the effects of green imperfections.

When a golfer walks on a green, a string of footprints are left behind. When the golfer addresses the ball, his feet push around, grinding into the grass and pressing down. When the green is wet and soft, the indentations can be relatively deep. For an average foursome, the number of footprints left on the green can exceed five hundred.

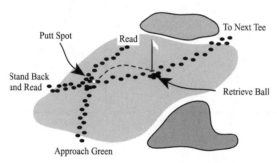

Not shown in the figure is the fact that the greatest clustering of footprints is closest to the hole because all golfers end up there at some point (hopefully).

Let's add lumps and pits to our computer model and see what happens. We will go back to our original condition of perfect putting and a perfect ball so that errors result only from green imperfections. The placement of the lumps and pits are random, just like footprints.

Lumpy greens provide another random element exactly like the wobbly golf ball. The effect is to

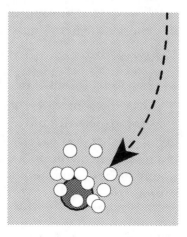

It is a thousand pities that neither Aristotle nor Shakespeare was a golfer. There is no other game that strips the soul so naked.

Horace Hutchinson

create clustering that is centered shorter of the hole, since riding the lumps steals momentum from the ball.

The problem is worse when the ball is traveling slowly, when the relative effects of momentum are less able to overcome impediments. Unfortunately the ball is traveling the slowest nearest the hole which means that this type of imperfection is one of the most influential, more so even than a lumpy ball.

Evidence of Lumpy Green Effects

In order to see just how much the greens really affect putts, I went to two different golf courses and did some testing. I used a putting ramp to eliminate human error; I used brand new balls to eliminate golf ball error, and I repeated the experiments enough times to get confidence in the results.

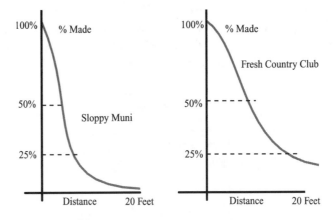

As you can see, making a putt under some conditions takes more luck than skill. You would expect lumpier greens at a municipal course, and sure enough the results demonstrate just that. You get what you pay for, in many ways, on a golf course. In general, the better golf courses have better greens.

Volcano

The worst problem of all occurs closest to the hole.

Over the course of a day, many golfers walk over the green. For obvious reasons, most of them walk near the hole. When a golfer reaches over to retrieve his ball from the hole, he tends to put his weight on one foot when he bends over, generally around twenty inches from the hole. This squashes the grass down, as shown.

Chance is a name for our ignorance.

Leslie Stephens

The Art and Science of Putting

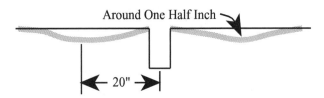

Around One Half Inch

← 20" →

In three dimensions this ramp looks like a volcano surrounded by a round valley. As the ball approaches the hole, there is also a ramp down to the bottom of the valley, so the net result is a ramp down, followed by a ramp up.

The volcano is especially bad at the end of the day and/or when the grass is wet. Some grass types spring back more quickly than others.

Let's go back to the computer model and see what happens when we include a volcano. We also want to include a little human error, since a perfect volcano will deflect a perfect putt the same way each time.

Imagine a larger hole. How would this affect the speed of play? How would this affect course design? How would this effect the volcano? How about scores?

The volcano tends to deflect the ball away from the hole, much like a magnet pushing away a steel ball. Note the donut shaped clustering. This is far different than the random, "dart board" clustering that we saw before. If the putt is ever so slightly off center (and almost all putts are), the volcano will increase the error and push the ball away from the hole.

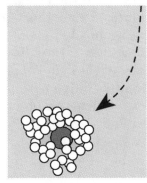

In essence, the effect of the volcano is to magnify errors.

The computer also suggests that the way to overcome the volcano is to putt with authority since momentum will overcome the effects of the volcano. This of course means that you will be looking at more difficult second putts (and third and fourth putts).

You Are a Better Putter Than You Thought

True reality consists of all of the errors put together — not to mention some more that have not even been named yet. We

When people say the greens are too fast, let them look to their own putting and see if the fault does not lie there.

Bernard Darwin

could run some more computer simulations that included all the errors, but you already know what will happen: major clustering.

You can now understand why you are a better putter than you thought you were. It is now understandable why your putting stroke is better in the morning than the afternoon, or why your putting is better on an expensive golf course. It is not uncommon on a municipal course for the volcano to get so bad that it is almost impossible to make a putt from any distance.

Optimum Aggression

It is of interest to study the optimum distance past the hole to aim for. It's usually not the case that the hole itself is the target (at least for the tour pros; most amateurs do aim for the hole). Pros generally aim for a point behind the hole, thereby reducing the effect of "never up, never in."

To look at this issue, we need to change tactics with our computer program. Instead of looking at paths and shot clusters, we will count how many putts it takes to sink the ball from a given spot on a green. We take the first putt, aiming somewhere at a spot directly past the hole. Sometimes this first putt will go into the hole for an ace. If not, we take the next shot from the first resting point, again aiming somewhere past the hole. Sometimes we make this second shot, and sometimes not. When not, we again take a shot. Then we repeat this process one thousand times and take statistics on the number of putts required. We can add any kind of imperfections we want, and we can study all kinds of different situations. Computers are ideal for repeating experiments an obscene number of times, and this is what we will do.

The following figure indicates the best odds:

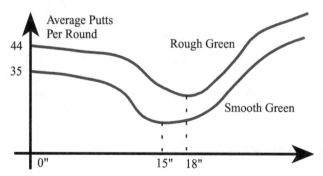

The best distance seems to be around eighteen inches on a rough green and fifteen inches on a smooth green. The figure

The Art and Science of Putting

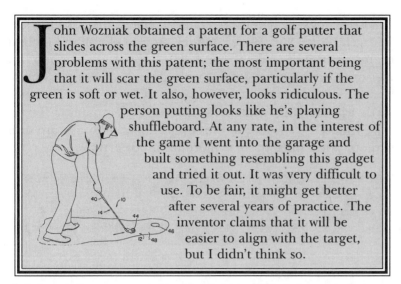

John Wozniak obtained a patent for a golf putter that slides across the green surface. There are several problems with this patent; the most important being that it will scar the green surface, particularly if the green is soft or wet. It also, however, looks ridiculous. The person putting looks like he's playing shuffleboard. At any rate, in the interest of the game I went into the garage and built something resembling this gadget and tried it out. It was very difficult to use. To be fair, it might get better after several years of practice. The inventor claims that it will be easier to align with the target, but I didn't think so.

also shows that very rough greens may result in as many as seven more strokes per round of golf; this is a large number.

Note that an assumption is in effect here which may be a very poor assumption. Most golfers seem to have far more trouble with shorter putts than they really should. We have all seen golfers that routinely miss three footers, while sinking every eight footer in sight. If you get the jitters at three feet, you may be better off aiming right for the hole since this will minimize the average distance to expect for your second putt.

What if the billiard swing was legal. Do you think it would be more accurate, and therefore used more often than the standard putt swing? Do you agree that the USGA should make rules because of the way things "look?"

Now the real question is not how to avoid three-putts at all cost, but how to minimize the number of putts in a round of eighteen holes (assuming stroke play). For instance, suppose a conservative strategy results in eighteen two putts; 36 total. An aggressive strategy results in thirteen two-putts, one three-putt and four one putts; a total of 33. Aggressive wins by three strokes.

Most beginners desperately seek to avoid three-putting and as a result they leave too many putts short of the hole. The pain of an occasional three-putt should be more than offset by the joy of a few one-putts. It is noteworthy how rare this attitude really is; human nature seems to dread failure far more than it enjoys success.

Sam Snead used a putter named the "croquet putter" near the end of his career. As its name suggests, it was suspended directly in front of his body and swung with one hand as a fixed point and the other hand providing the force. This putter style was later outlawed because it looked bad; no other reason.

This brings up another related subject, that of targeting approach shots. Suppose we model a round of golf in which we aim toward the low side of the hole (as opposed to right at the hole, or at the high side). Now we will enjoy more uphill putts, although the average length of a putt may be greater. The question is whether this strategy works out to fewer putts for the entire round. According to the computer, uphill putts are sunk far more often since there is more room for error.

> What would happen to the game if there were no putting, just a round, horizontal net of some given size, perhaps ten feet in diameter. When the ball landed in the net, the hole was finished. Surely the best golfers in the world would be different than the ones we have now. What would happen to your score (in relation to other golfers, that is)?

How well do the pros do?

OK, enough theory for now. Let's jump into reality by taking a look at how well the tour pros do. While we might expect a lot from ourselves, it would be foolish to expect to putt better than the pros. Remember that the pros get to putt on the best greens, so the lumps are minimal and the volcanoes are usually nonexistent. The number of players or caddies that go near the cup is much more limited than it would be at a Sunday muni. Debris is swept away and the greens are flattened and mowed to a fine precision. In other words, the pros see the best conditions that are likely to be seen. Not only that, but they use a brand new ball for one or two holes at most, so they virtually eliminate golf ball imperfections. Here are the statistics on putting from the tour.

The fifty percent point is only at around six feet. 25% is at around ten feet. The next time you line up a six footer, remember the tour pros only make half of them. If you make one out of three you are probably doing as well as you can expect, given the worse conditions you are likely experiencing.

Next time you play golf, write down the lengths of your putts and after a few rounds, calculate your percentages. It might be interesting to do this for uphill, downhill, right to left and other categories as well.

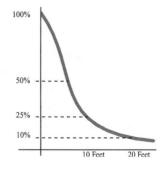

Making Contact

5

Golf Balls

The maximum weight of a golf ball is 1.62 ounces (45.93 grams). A heavier ball, if legal, would travel further in the air because it would barrel through the wind resistance with more momentum. On the putting surface, a heavier ball would barrel through the pits and lumps with less deviation. Since there is no good reason to make the ball lighter than the maximum, manufacturers try to achieve the maximum.

The minimum diameter of a golf ball is 1.68 inches (42.67 mm). A smaller ball would experience less wind resistance, but would be more susceptible to the bumps and lumps of a green. Sometimes when you see an advertisement in the back of a golf magazine offering golf balls with amazing distance, they are simply the smaller balls that are used in Japan and Europe. If you decide to use one, remember that you get a distance advantage, but a ground-game disadvantage.

The maximum initial velocity is 250 feet per second (76.2 meters per second), which is measured at the output of a standard ball striking machine, something like the "Iron Byron" which you see in commercials.

Suppose the initial velocity specification were changed, either upward or downward. It would stand to reason that the size of the average golf course would have to be scaled accordingly, everything else being equal.

Golf ball construction may be divided into four categories:

1) One piece ball
2) Two piece ball
3) Three piece ball
4) Balata ball (now made of a mixture of natural balata and synthetic rubbers)

The ball doesn't care how positive you are thinking when you hit it with a putter that is moving and aimed in the wrong direction.

Dave Pelz

33

From a putting standpoint, there is little difference between the balls, although each offers a characteristic "feel" as it is struck by the putter.

In putting, the density profile of the ball is of some interest, as a ball with a center of gravity which does not match the physical center will tend to wobble and roll erratically. The one piece ball retains the best symmetry over its lifetime, and the balata ball the least.

The cover material of a golf ball determines the feel it will have as the putter strikes it. Many people choose their golf balls for this very reason. Cover materials react differently to hot and cold and humidity. Icy cold, one-piece balls sound and feel like a piece of rock when they are struck by a putter. The "moment of inertia" varies for each ball type. This is a physical term related to the ball's angular momentum (that momentum due to rotation). We all know what the word momentum means; the heavier a body is, the more difficult it is to start or stop. Angular momentum is the equivalent concept for a spinning object.

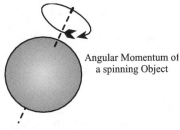

Angular Momentum of a spinning Object

The weight is essentially the same for each ball, but it is possible to pack a higher density material into the center of a multi-piece ball, and so make the moment of inertia smaller.

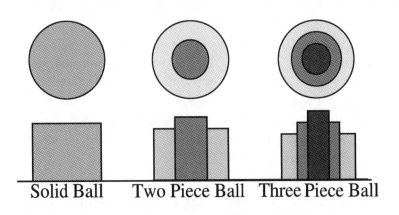

Solid Ball   Two Piece Ball   Three Piece Ball

The Art and Science of Putting

This results in greater spin, which is one of the reasons why balata balls stick to the green so well on approaches.

The compression number of a ball is related to its elasticity; a higher compression means a higher speed upon impact. Although it does not affect putting as much as the full swing, higher compression also means less time on the clubface, which means less spin.

The compression specification is more relative than objective. It is difficult to compare 90 compression balls from different manufacturers, although a group of balls from the same manufacturer should behave very much the same.

The following table shows the results of some testing done on the putting green with different balls. Each ball was hit with the same putting machine, with the exact same swing.

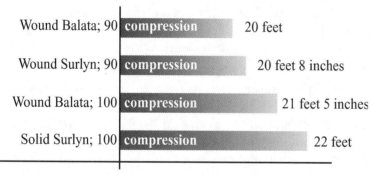

Wound Balata; 90 compression	20 feet
Wound Surlyn; 90 compression	20 feet 8 inches
Wound Balata; 100 compression	21 feet 5 inches
Solid Surlyn; 100 compression	22 feet

According to the test results, there is around 7% difference in the length from 90 to 100 compression. (This is only valid for putting.)

It should be clear that using a 90 compression ball on one green, and then a 100 compression ball on the next green will lead to problems with distance, more so on longer putts than short. In fact, you should use the same type of ball throughout the round, and you should also use the same balls on the practice green before the round. If you use some old 90's on the practice green and then open a new sleeve of 100's on the first tee, you will likely hit your putts well past the hole until you get used to the new compression. This problem is made worse by the fact that most practice greens are of poorer quality than course greens, and so take a harder stroke regardless of the ball. It makes more sense to use a 100 compression on the practice green, and a 90 on the course.

Ball compression also changes with temperature. Here is some data that shows the extent of the problem.

Golf is a game of emotion. If you can't control your emotions, you can't play golf.

Ben Hogan

Making Contact

Distance	Temp	Change
22.6	105	+3%
22.4	95	+2%
22.2	85	+1%
22.0	75	0
21.6	65	-2%
21.4	55	-3%
20.5	45	-7%
19.6	35	-12%

As you can see, there is not too much difference until the temperature starts to get below 55. This is not really that cold. The heat conductivity of golf ball covers is very low, which means that the temperature does not change very fast. If you stick a cold ball into your pocket, it will take a long time for it to warm up. Likewise, if you stick some previously warmed golf balls into your pocket before you begin your round, they will stay warm for a long time.

Finally, the dimple pattern is of little importance in putting. While the pattern influences the lift characteristics of a ball (and likewise its propensity to slice and hook), the dimples have a negligible influence on putting performance. If there were no dimples, the ball would be like a cue ball, which would work just fine.

Ball Line versus Target Line

We need to define two different but related concepts:

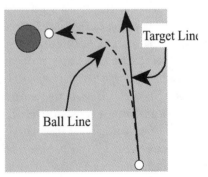

The ball line is the path the ball follows throughout its roll (almost always a curve), and the target line is always a straight, imaginary line to which the golfer has chosen to putt the ball. It is exactly on top of the ball line right at the point of impact. When you decide that there is nine inches of break, your target

The Art and Science of Putting

line goes from the position of your ball to nine inches to the side of the cup.

Target lines are pictured in many different ways. Some golfers like to imagine a spot several feet in front of their ball, and they try to putt over that spot. Other golfers can picture the imaginary line itself in their minds.

Since there are always a range of ways to accomplish a putt (see Chapter 4), there are many potential ball lines to the hole. The target line establishes the choice.

Putter Path Versus Angle of Impact

The putter path is the path that the putter follows as it progresses through the swing. It begins behind the ball, and then it goes backwards and then forward, through the ball.

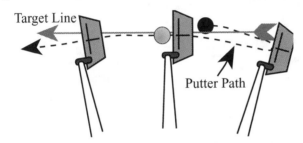

It should be obvious that the only time the putter path matters is *right* when it is striking the ball. This is true for the full swing as well, where golfers such as Lee Trevino in particular seem to have very awkward swing paths, but obviously they have things under control right at the point of impact.

At the point of impact, there are two fundamental alignments that affect the direction the ball goes when it is struck. The first is obviously the putter path, but the second is much more significant. It is the angle of the putter face, or angle of impact.

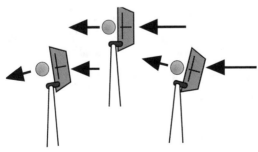

The greatest mistake you can make in this life is to be continually fearing you will make one.

Elbert Hubbard

Making Contact

Based on a wide range of empirical data, the ratio of influence is around 15% putter path to 85% angle of impact. The angle of impact is around 5 times more important.

This figure shows how the angle of impact affects the ball line.

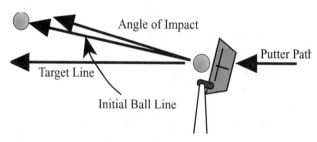

This figure shows how the putter path affects the ball line.

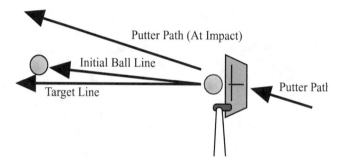

Many beginners worry exclusively about putter path. They watch the putter as it goes back and forth and they try to match the path to the target line. They are missing the real issue. Besides, trying to be so mechanical always causes poor putting because it takes too much concentration away from the intuition.

The following figure shows another fallacy of the effort to keep the putter on the target line. A normal backswing comes "inside" a little bit, as shown:

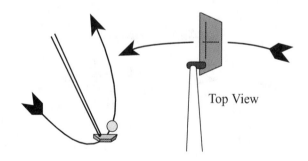

This naturally results in the putter head moving inside the target line. Trying too hard to keep the putter head directly over the target line results in unnatural movement.

Loft

A putter has a small amount of loft built into the face, somewhere on the order of four degrees, more or less. Some putters are flat and some have more than six degrees.

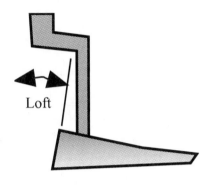

Loft

This is only part of the story, however. Loft can also be affected by the position of the hands at the point of impact.

Here the loft is actually negative, or facing down into the grass because the hands are far ahead of the putter face at the point of impact.

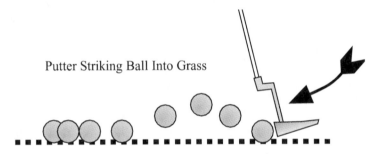

Putter Striking Ball Into Grass

On the contrary, here is what happens when the hands are behind the putter face at the point of impact.

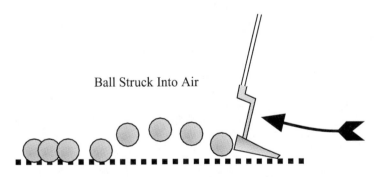

Ball Struck Into Air

Any negative loft is detrimental, and a small amount of positive loft is advantageous or irrelevant.

Putter Physics

6

Putter Types

Putters generally fall into one of two categories: blade putters and center-shafted putters. If the shaft intersects the clubhead at one of the ends, it is a blade putter, and if it intersects near the center it is a center-shafted putter.

It is also possible to categorize putters by their head styles. The straight blade is a thin, light-weight head that is used for fast greens and a deft touch. The flange blade is a straight blade with an extension added to the back of the clubhead to increase the mass. The mallet head is larger and generally rounder.

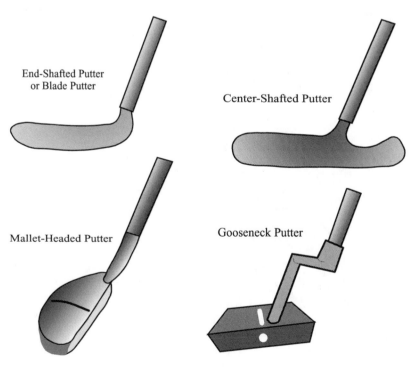

End-Shafted Putter
or Blade Putter

Center-Shafted Putter

Mallet-Headed Putter

Gooseneck Putter

Bobby Jones named his putter Calamity Jane. This is a prime example of the emotion that many golfers have for their putters.

Putter Standards

	Loft	Lie	Length	Weight
Less	2.0°	69°	32"	10.0 oz
Average	4.0°	74°	36"	11.5 oz
More	6.0°	79°	>37"	13.0 oz

Sweet Spot

Every putter has a unique "sweet spot." It's the spot on the clubface that you want to use to hit the ball. It's easy enough to find.

Suspend Putter
Loosely in
Fingertips

Tap Golf Ball Lightly
Onto Clubface

Hold the putter as shown, and tap the putter-face with a golf ball until the strike is clean and does not cause sideway twitching or twisting on the shaft.

Most putters have a small alignment mark located on top of the clubface, somewhere near the center of the face.

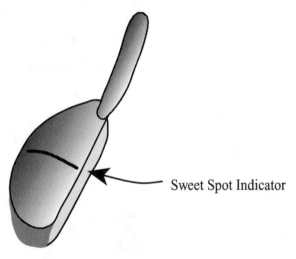

Sweet Spot Indicator

Jack Nicklaus used an oversized putter named The Response ZT to win the 1986 Masters. Sales of the putter soared after the tournament.

The Art and Science of Putting

This is almost always aligned with the sweet spot. To be sure, you still need to do the experiment shown above.

When you strike the ball directly on the sweet spot, the impact will feel finely tuned, like a nice click.

The importance of the sweet spot varies from putter to putter. Basically, if you hit the ball away from the sweet spot, the putter will twist away from the putt, momentarily diverting the angle of impact.

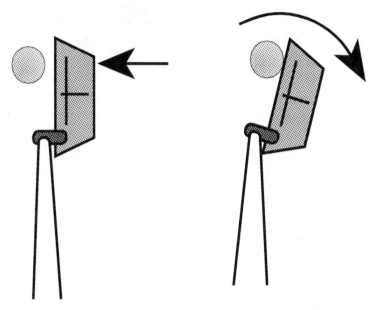

Some putters are more forgiving than others in this regard. In general, heavier, larger-faced putters are more forgiving since their moment of inertia is larger. The greater effect of missing the sweet spot may be psychological since it detracts from the nice, clean feel.

It is possible to define the "width" of the sweet spot.

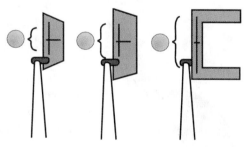

Note that the putter on the right side was designed specifically to maximize the width of the sweet spot. This is done by moving the mass away (equally on both sides) from the sweet spot itself. Also, by extending the mass toward the rear, this effect is amplified.

You can find out if you are hitting at the sweet spot by attaching a pair of rubber bands onto the putter face.

If you hit one of the rubber bands the ball will fly off at an angle and you will feel a rubbery thump instead of a nice click.

If you are erratic or inconsistent in your striking spot, you should try to practice until you do not hit the rubber bands anymore.

Keep in mind that, although the sweet spot is important, it should not consume your attention while you are putting. You can certainly hit the sweet spot without sinking a putt, just as you can make a putt without hitting the sweet spot. In fact, it would not be difficult to find an excellent putter who rarely hits the sweet spot.

Changing the Sweet Spot

If you never are able to hit your putter's sweet spot and cannot stand the thought of getting rid of "Ol' Bess," you can fix her up by strategically adding some lead tape to the rear and bottom of the clubface.

Not only will this move the sweet spot and adjust the balance, it will also increase the "width" of the sweet spot, or the ability of the putter to tolerate mis-hits.

Place Lead Weight Equally About the Sweet Spot

Adding tape also increases the weight of the clubhead, and most people are sensitive to this kind of change. It should be intuitive that changing the weight will change the club's natural tempo.

A club hung freely and swung like a pendulum will have a natural period of oscillation. The heavier the club (technically speaking, the weight distribution is important as well), the longer it takes to swing back and forth. In the process of swinging, the hands and muscles force the club back and forth through its swing path. The greater the difference between the natural tempo of the club and the desired tempo of the golfer (a mental attitude), the more activity the golfer must apply.

Most golfers would benefit from a heavier club because it forces patience. It is a natural tendency, both in putting and the fairway game, to "jerk" into the forward part of the swing before the backswing is nicely finished. A heavier club will force a slower, smoother tempo (to a point, of course).

The tape is legal, as long as it is not removed or applied during a round.

Lie

The lie of a putter is defined as follows:

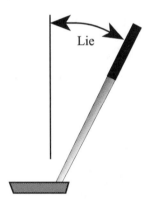

There does not appear to be any reason to insist on one lie more than another, but the lie affects your posture and stance (more on this later). In fact it is rare that a lie doesn't fit the golfer, because most golfers choose a putter for its lie and length (and appearance).

If you watch other golfers, you will see all kinds of lies. This is attributable to the fact that everybody has a preferred posture, ranging from very low to practically straight up. Putting is clearly more individualistic than the full-swing game in this regard.

While awkward-looking lies abound, it matters not. If awkward-looking were a realistic criterion for great putting, Lee Trevino might be slinging hamburgers in a Texas grill.

Experts who have studied the matter assure us that the mind can only think of one thing at a time. Obviously they have never made a study of golfers, or they would lower their estimate.

Robinson Murray

Weight

The total weight of the head is of some importance, but not much. If it were too light, it would be like hitting a basketball with a baseball bat; the bat bounces off the ball more than the ball bounces off the bat. On the other hand, imagine a putter head of extreme weight. It would be too unwieldy to handle, especially for the shorter putts.

For the most part, weight is nonessential. You need to choose a weight you are comfortable with, no more, no less. It is probably true that using a light-weight blade is better on very fast greens since the smaller weight lends itself to more finesse and touch. But if you don't like a blade, it will do no good under any circumstances.

A heavier clubface will usually result in a more forgiving sweet spot, and as already mentioned, a heavier club will force patience.

Keep in mind that you can always add lead tape to your putter, and in fact, you should probably try it sometime just to see what happens. It doesn't cost much and it will make you more aware of the universe of possibilities. Anything you do that will make you more aware of the game can only help.

Loft

Loft is defined as follows:

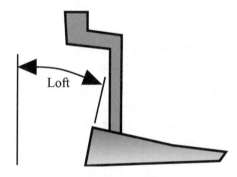

In the last chapter we looked at what happens during the ball striking process due to variations in loft. You need to decide if your hands tend to go forward or backward of the clubface when you strike the ball.

Shape

Here we get to the most subjective aspect of a putter. In fact, shape is the aspect which has the least influence on effec-

The Art and Science of Putting

tiveness, at least from a physics standpoint. Ironically it is shape that sells more putters than any other factor.

The width of the sweet spot varies with shape, since a more distributed weight distribution creates a higher moment of inertia.

Putters come in as many varieties of shape as there are manufacturers. Some are painted black, some silver, some are even red. No matter.

Some are shaped like eggs, some like tubes and some are shaped like an alien spacecraft. No matter. The most interesting diversity of appearance concerns the alignment lines and devices. And in this case, whatever works well for you is the best. Some people visualize parallel lines better.

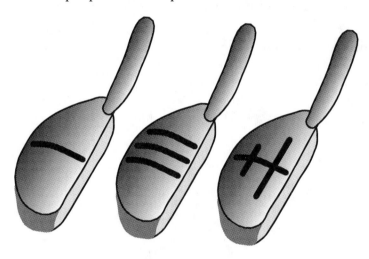

Some prefer perpendicular lines. Sometimes angular structures seem to work. If you like a certain shape more than another, that is reason enough. You will be much better with a putter you like than one that you don't.

But keep in mind that some shapes violate the physical conditions established previously. If you are going to choose a putter by its appearance, just make sure it passes the following tests first:

1) Sweet spot around the center of the face
2) Balance is good
3) Length (may be modified) is correct for your posture and height
4) Loft is adequate for your style

It would be hoped one's head might be put to greater use than a convenient place to hang one's hat.

Steven Corie

Plumb Bobbing

Plumb bobbing is the technique of reading slope while holding your putter up in front of yourself. There are certain fundamentals of bobbing which must be done properly for the technique to have any value.

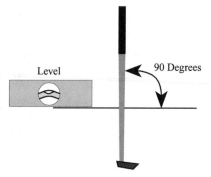

The idea is simple. The putter shaft hangs straight down, thereby giving the viewer an idea of true level. At this point, true level is exactly perpendicular to the putter shaft, so a certain amount of visualization is required. Specifically, you must visualize a line perpendicular to the putter shaft.

First, let's take a look at finding the true vertical of a putter shaft. As you rotate the putter in your fingers, you will see it turn, as follows:

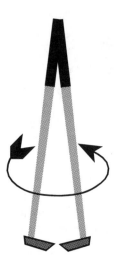

The putter actually transcribes a cone, unless the shaft hangs straight down under the grip, which is rare (for this to happen, the weight distribution of the clubface must be perfectly symmetric about the shaft). In addition, the shaft tapers from the grip to the head, so even if the shaft is hanging straight down, the side of the shaft may be skewed.

The Art and Science of Putting

The trick is to find the orientation which will make the shaft (one side or the other) appear vertical from your vantage point. The best way to do this is to find a truly vertical wall or beam and then stand away and plumb bob as you would on a green.

Once you have found the proper orientation, make sure you always hold the putter in that manner when you plumb bob.

The real problem is one of visualization. You are not really interested in true vertical, but true level, or true horizontal, and plumb bobbing can only give you true vertical. Some people are better at mental geometry than others. Empirical testing has shown that most humans can see a ninety degree angle to within a few degrees, so trust yourself.

A Texas Wedge refers to a putter used from off a green. The name comes from the fact that golf courses in Texas are very dry and firm in the summer, making the fringe and outlying areas quite flat and predictable.

Reading Greens

7

Art Versus Science

The practice of reading greens is an excellent example of the balance between science and intuition. Reading various physical characteristics of a green involves sensory observation, but the final product is an intuitive "feel."

Reading a green and making a decision on how and where to hit the putt are indistinguishable. One does not "read" a green, then make a decision; the read and decision are one and the same.

Suppose we could measure, using scientific instrumentation, every physical aspect of a green and its surroundings. The result of our measurements would be a table of data. For instance, we could measure all the different slopes and thereby make up a contour map with as much detail as we wanted. We could then measure the speed (the friction) and the amount of lumpiness, and we could easily measure the wind speed and direction. Now suppose that we have a putting machine that we can accurately program. We know the physics of the ball contact, and we know the physics of the ball roll. We could apply our physics equations and set up our machine and plug away.

How often would we sink a putt this way? An even more interesting question is how would our machine process compare to a tour pro?

While the pro would be subject to human error, the machine process would also miss plenty of putts, but for a different reason. The simple fact is that not every aspect of a green may be measured with hard instrumentation. Human senses have far more depth than an entire array of machines and instruments. In a single glance, we are able to digest a situation and make a decision. Of course if we take our time and carefully study dif-

Show me a man with both feet planted firmly on the ground and I'll show you a man about to swing a golf club.

Bing Crosby

ferent perspectives, our decisions will be better. The point is that we can do an amazingly good job with the tools God gave us.

Start Early

Reading a green involves two "assessments." The first is an attempt to gauge (mentally absorb) the sloping contours. The second is a judgment of the speed of the green and the other conditions analyzed in Chapter 4.

Optimal Fact: As you approach a green it is easier to get a relative feeling for the general slope from a distance. Perception of true level is much better from a distance because the eyes are able to take in more information that way. You can see trees and hills and clouds and maybe some water. When you are right on top of a green, you can only see the green.

Many amateurs hit their approach shots and then wander toward the green without paying much attention. Good putting begins when you first see the green.

Sometimes as you are playing a round of golf, you can see greens in adjacent fairways before you end up playing that hole. You cannot only do a little advance green reading, but you can also take a look at where the flag is and consider where you would like to hit your ball at that hole.

Green reading is an art of awareness and assessment, not a science of measurement and analysis.

Go All Around

Another simple fact is that the more vantages you can witness, the better your read. Take your time, take a deep breath and absorb.

Watch the pros on Sunday and you will see them walk not just behind their ball, but to the sides and all around the green. They are not gathering facts; they are gathering feel.

Plumb Bobbing

Plumb bobbing is good for telling which way a green breaks. The best vantage for the technique is to be down close to the green's surface. This makes it easier to see the surface in relation to the vertically hanging putter shaft.

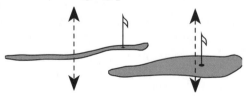

Natural golfers are bad golfers but natural putters are good putters.

Percy Boomer

The Art and Science of Putting

The figure on the left is easier to read for slope than the figure on the right because the read is done down closer to the surface of the green. You can either bend over or rest on your knee, or if possible stand back from the green and find a dip in the terrain that will allow you to get your head more level with the green surface.

Raised greens should be easier to read than sunken surfaces since it is easier to get down to the surface. Nothing says you can't walk away from the green surface, even up to twenty or more yards. This will enable you to get a worm's eye view of the surface.

Water

Reading a green's slope requires a reference to what is really level. When there is water near a green, this can often provide the best possible reference, since the surface of the water is perfectly level.

Look out over the water and try to use it to establish a sense of level. You may find this to be difficult if the water is at a lower elevation or if the surface is not smooth, but it should provide you with some guidance. Remember, establishing an idea of level is an intuitive process. The more you practice it, the better you will become. Trust yourself. If you try to be scientific about it, it won't work.

Closest to the Hole Matters Most

As you will recall, the chapter on the physics of a rolling golf ball presented a series of roll trajectories. Most of the curvature was near the end of the roll, which should occur close to the hole. Therefore, it is the influence of the slope nearest the hole that matters the most.

The place to begin drawing potential ball paths is not from the ball to the hole, but from the hole to the ball. Most golfers do this backwards, although if the read is accurate, it doesn't matter. Beware of using the flagstick as a level reference. There is absolutely no reason why the flagstick should be vertical, and it almost always hangs to one side or the other. In fact, the flagstick may actually create an optical illusion that will skew your intuitive sense of the level plane. Take it out of the hole and try reading the green.

I never pray on the golf course. Actually, the Lord answers my prayers everywhere except on the course.

Rev. Billy Graham

It is amazing how well the human comprehension can tackle the job of reading a green. Trust yourself, and when there is a problem, first look for the fault somewhere else besides your read. Even then, the best of the best often misread. When the TV commentators attach blame to a pro's missed putt, they love to say that the green was "misread." How can they make that conclusion? Probably because they can't stand the thought that the pros could be guilty of poor mechanics. On the other hand, it is very common for many pros to miss a hole exactly the same way on a given day. This is probably due to misreading. There seems to be a challenge by the greenskeepers to try to trick the pros by insidious pin placements and tricky settings. There are things that create optical illusions such as placing a pin against a background of trees that have been pushed over from the wind. Trees generally grow straight up, or approximately so, but when there is a prevailing wind they will lean away from the wind in an attempt to find relief. This is very common along coastlines.

Reading Grain

Just like slope, grain will affect the curvature of the ball when it is close to the hole. It is usually easy to see the grain right at the hole by looking down into the cut edges of the hole.

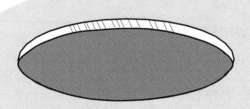

Judging the direction of grain is not usually a problem, but judging the magnitude of the effect is. Sometimes it is possible to read grain by dragging the back of your putter across the grass. When you drag with the grain, the putter will move smoothly. When you drag against the grain, the putter will catch and hesitate and the grass will snag upward.

Another method of determining the grain of the grass is looking to see how it appears in light. If the grain is against you, the grass will appear lighter. It is with you, it will look darker. This is why freshly mowed grass has the appearance of stripes of alternating light and dark (made by the alternating mower paths).

Reading Lumps and the Volcano

While lumps and volcanoes may be relatively easy to see and read, the only thing you can do about them when putting is to turn up the aggression a notch. There is no way to read the severity or the magnitude of the lumps to a degree that would be useful.

You can read the surface of a green oftentimes by simply feeling how it sinks when you walk over it. Softer greens will naturally have worse lumps and volcanoes, but it depends on what time of day it is. If you are out first thing in the morning the lumps should not be bad.

Most putts are missed because of mis-hitting, not because of mireading. Missing the sweet spot on the putter face is a more common reason for missed putts than misreading.

Reading Speed

You can use the plumb bob method to judge how much uphill or downhill your putt is. As you will recall, the plumb bob method is used to measure level. When you stand behind your ball and plumb bob, you can see the sideward slope that the ball will experience. This will tell you if the ball is going to break right or left, and if you are good, you will be able to tell how much. If you stand off to the side of your putt, instead of behind it or in front of it, you will be able to see if the putt is uphill or downhill, and if you are good, you will be able to tell how much.

You can also tell how hard a green is by the way it feels as you walk, although this is a pretty loose way to make a decision. The best way to read the speed of a green is to go out on the practice green before your round begins. You must then hope that the greens on the course are the same, which is not always the case.

Drainage Gives Insight

Most greens are designed with adequate drainage in mind. Greens are watered almost every night. If there were no route

A good spectator also creates.

Swiss Proverb

Reading Greens

55

for the water to drain from the surface, puddles would form and soft spots would then appear like freckles around the green.

You can usually see the drainage pattern of a green by observing the flow of grain. Grass grain generally tends to follow the drainage pattern, and of course since water finds the lowest level, the slope of the green will be apparent from the drainage pattern as well.

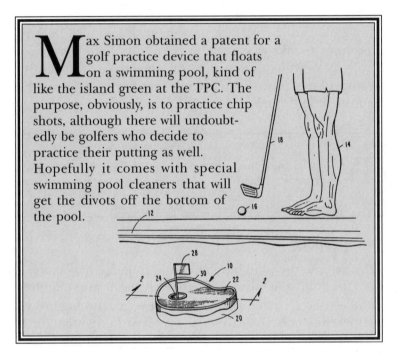

Max Simon obtained a patent for a golf practice device that floats on a swimming pool, kind of like the island green at the TPC. The purpose, obviously, is to practice chip shots, although there will undoubtedly be golfers who decide to practice their putting as well. Hopefully it comes with special swimming pool cleaners that will get the divots off the bottom of the pool.

Putting Machines

8

Introduction

In this chapter, we are going to examine a few machines that are capable of putting a golf ball in order to demonstrate the importance of simplicity. A good putting stroke should be very simple. Many problems that golfers experience can be related to unwarranted complexity.

Machine I: Simple Ramp

The simplest and cheapest "putting" machine is an inclined ramp.

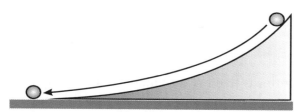

This machine is consistent and reliable. It has the further advantage that the ball is rolling (rotating) when it hits the putting surface. This does not occur with a ball striking machine which hits a stationary ball (a swinging putter in other words). The speed is easily adjusted by changing the position of the ball, and it is also easy to aim; a gunsight could be used for this purpose. The cross-hairs would be aimed right down the target line.

The best use for such a device is to measure the speed of a green. A ball is allowed to roll down the ramp, onto the green surface, and the total distance that the ball rolls is then mea-

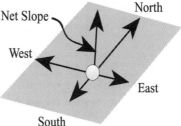

From such crooked wood as that which man is made of, nothing straight can be fashioned.

Kant

57

sured. The ball is started at a standardized point on the ramp so that the exit speed is always the same. The result is a subjective measurement that may be used to compare different greens on different courses. A green that measures twenty feet is faster than a green that measures fifteen feet.

The ramp may also be used to measure slope. This is done by measuring the roll distance in four different directions.

Using the standard rules of vector algebra, the four measurements are combined into a single value that will yield the net slope. This method is not as accurate as a carpenter's level placed on a green surface, however, and the level is far easier to use.

Unfortunately the ramp does very little by way of instruction since the point is to study machines in comparison to the human body. We need a machine that swings a club.

Machine II: Simple Rotator

Here is the simplest machine that actually swings a club:

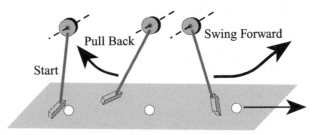

The putter is fixed to a rotatable ball bearing arrangement mounted to a rigid stand (the stand is not included in the figure). The putter is swung by pulling it back, as shown, and then letting it go. This is far more accurate than giving it a push since it is very difficult to judge how hard to push. A gunsight may be used to aim down the target line, and the speed is adjusted by varying how far back the putter is pulled.

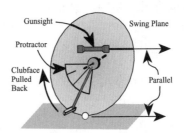

It is instructive to study how the putter path changes as the swing plane is moved around.

This figure shows a vertical swing plane.

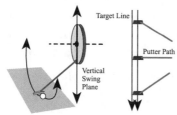

The putter path is always parallel to the target line (or on top of the target line to be more exact). If the putter face is perpendicular to the target line at the point of the ball, it will remain so throughout the swing. Therefore, the ball will be hit right down the target line. The vertical swing plane is very simple and efficient.

Now in this figure the swing plane is inclined backward.

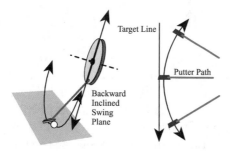

The putter path goes inside of the target line on both the backswing and the forward swing. The putter face "opens" on the backswing and closes on the forward part of the swing. At the point of impact the putter path is exactly parallel to the target line and the putter face is exactly perpendicular to the target line.

This orientation is not bad since it hits the ball properly, but it is more difficult to use than the vertical swing plane. To understand this, suppose the machine moved a little forward or backward during the swing (which is how a human body often moves). The putt will no longer go down the target line because the putter path would be shifted back and forth as well.

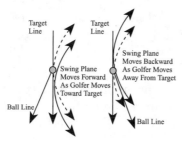

Putting Machines

The player may experiment about his swing, his grip, his stance. It is only when he begins asking his caddie's advice that he is getting on dangerous ground.

Sir Walter Simpson

This suggests a potential for problems because it is difficult to hold perfectly still during a swing. Putters who have an awkward swing plane say that their key to putting is to hold perfectly still. You can understand why. Of course if the swing plane is vertical, this problem does not arise.

Now in this figure the swing plane is inclined forward:

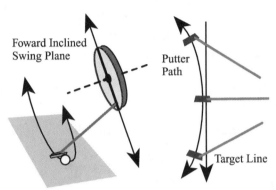

The putter path goes outside of the target line on both the backswing and the forward swing, and the putter face closes, then opens, as shown. This is the inverse of the backward inclined swing plane. It suffers the same problem as the backward inclination. If there is any movement by the golfer toward or away from the target during the swing, the ball will not be hit down the target line.

Here is what happens when the swing plane is "open" to the target line:

This results from aiming the machine to the left of the target.

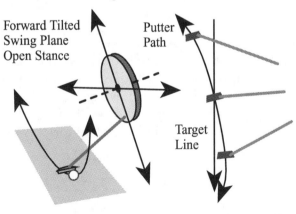

This "open" misalignment could be compensated by opening the putter face, since the clubface orientation is more important than the putter path. Sound complicated? It is, but

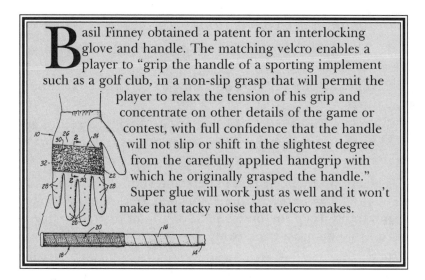

Basil Finney obtained a patent for an interlocking glove and handle. The matching velcro enables a player to "grip the handle of a sporting implement such as a golf club, in a non-slip grasp that will permit the player to relax the tension of his grip and concentrate on other details of the game or contest, with full confidence that the handle will not slip or shift in the slightest degree from the carefully applied handgrip with which he originally grasped the handle." Super glue will work just as well and it won't make that tacky noise that velcro makes.

there are golfers who line up crookedly, swing crookedly and make putts anyway. In fact, this kind of thing is relatively common, especially for amateurs. Many putters line up with their shoulders open to the target, which usually results in an open swing plane.

Finally, we can add some complexity that makes no sense from a machine standpoint, but is unfortunately the way many golfers swing.

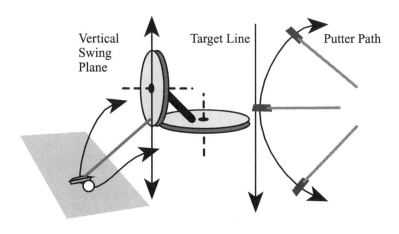

Vertical Swing Plane   Target Line   Putter Path

Now as the club swings back, the horizontal ball bearing arrangement also swings back, causing a very convoluted putter path. Instead of simply swinging on a nice arc, the putter path has become very complicated. For many golfers, this movement is the cause for many poor putting strokes.

Two Common Misconceptions

1) The clubface should be kept perpendicular to the target line at all times.

2) The putter path should be directly over the target line at all times.

Too many amateurs try to do both of these things and are aided in their attempts by dozens of products that are out on the market.

The important thing is to understand your own swing plane orientation. If your orientation is inclined forward or backward, attempting to keep the putter path on top of the target line is very detrimental to a good swing.

Putting is personal; you need to understand your own putting stroke and make it work for you. Machines are interesting to study because they demonstrate some of the physics of motion. They may be good models to try to copy, but the human body is simply too complicated a machine to adequately model. Besides, putting is mostly a mental process; if you feel comfortable with a certain putt stroke it will work well for you regardless of how many laws of physics you are violating. Again, the key is to understand what you are doing.

Ball Moved Forward/Backward in Stance

When the ball is moved backward in the stance, it is struck into the grass because the putter face is "de-lofted."

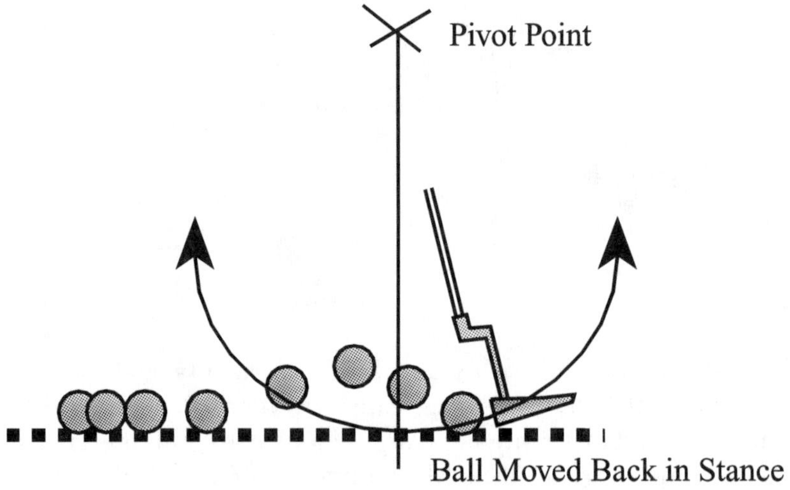

Pivot Point

Ball Moved Back in Stance

We can use the computer model from the earlier chapters and see what happens to the accuracy when this occurs.

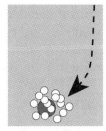

There is a certain amount of dispersion, or randomness, caused by this obvious mistake. Both the speed and direction have clustered, and the average length of the clustered shots is shorter as well. This is because some momentum is robbed from the ball when it is struck into the grass.

It may seem that changing to a higher lofted putter might remedy the problem, but this is not the case.

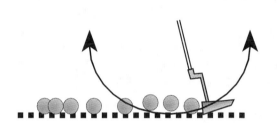
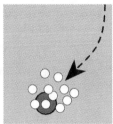

Even by compensating with a higher lofted putter, the results are poor. This indicates that the direction of movement, ie, downward into the grass at impact, is influential. This is no surprise; the putter path is 15% influential in terms of hitting to the target line. The same thing holds for hitting downward on the ball. In the full swing, hitting down on the ball is very desirable with shorter irons since it puts spin on the ball. Any attempt to impart backward spin on a putt makes no sense and should be avoided.

On the other hand, here is what happens when the pivot point is behind the clubface at impact:

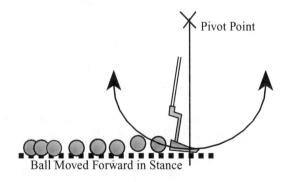

Pivot Point

Ball Moved Forward in Stance

The results are much better, in fact, there is no dispersion caused at all. The results do not start to cluster until the upward movement becomes very pronounced, and this is difficult to do at any rate. The obvious conclusion is that it will be far better to place the ball forward in the stance. The pivot point for a human is usually defined around the middle of the shoulders, so placing the ball near the left foot will provide a good starting point.

> Imagine a different game of golf. Suppose that it was legal and proper to bring any kind of machine that you wanted onto the golf course. You could even bring a four wheel drive truck which came equipped with special high-tech ball shooters. On the greens you could use laser rangefinders, gunsights and whatever else you could possibly think of.
>
> 1) Would Jack Nicklaus still be the best golfer of all time?
>
> 2) Would you simply prefer to play the old way?

Variation of Pivot Radius

By using a longer putter, the pivot point is raised to around six or seven feet above the surface. This changes the timing of the machine in an important way.

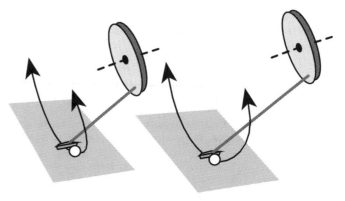

Charles Boswell of Birmingham, Alabama took up the sport of golf after being blinded by shellfire in World War II. He once shot a round of 81.

For both machines, the further back the putter is pulled prior to release, the harder it will hit the ball. For the longer machine, however, the timing of the swing is slower. The longer the putter, the more patience is required. If both machines are pulled back to a forty five degree angle, the longer putter will hit the ball further and it will also swing much slower. In this way it is more wieldy in terms of power. In the sense that putting is like tight-rope walking, the longer putters are the same as the stabilizing bars held by the walkers. They make balance very easy, but the tricks become harder.

The   Art   and   Science   of   Putting

The longer the putter the more difficult it is to get a feel for the speed. Nevertheless, the long putters have found considerable popularity, particularly among the seniors. Since patience and tempo are so important in putting, the real advantage in the longer putters may be that they force patience.

A Better Look at Aiming

The gunsight was used to align the machine with the target line.

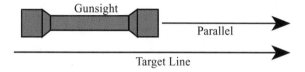

Gunsight

Parallel

Target Line

If we want the aiming mechanism to apply to putts of all lengths, the only possible mounting spot for the cross-hairs is directly above the target line.

Why? If the sighting tube is placed off to the side, it is necessary to know the distance to a point on the target line as well as the separation between the gunsight and the ball (or the target line).

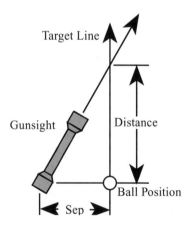

Target Line

Gunsight

Distance

Ball Position

Sep

A calculation is made using a calculator and some trigonometry equations. Of course this is absurd.

The obvious point is that the sighting is far more simple when it is done directly over the target line. While a human does not use a gunsight, the general idea still applies; the eyes should be poised directly over the target line.

Golf is an awkward set of bodily contortions designed to produce a graceful result.

Tommy Armour

> S uppose you could have a professional golf teacher accompany you on the golf course and give you advice at all times.
>
> 1) Would your scores be lower?
>
> 2) Would your mechanics be the same?
>
> 3) How long would it take before you were tired of this arrangement?

Machine III: Complex Rotator

The next machine is similar to the rotator, but it has another pivot point at the "wrist" position in addition to the "shoulder" pivot point.

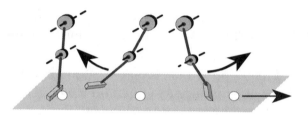

In theory, this machine could perform just as well as the simple rotator, but there is also no reason why it would perform any better. From a simplicity standpoint, it clearly offers no improvement. The real difference between the two machines is that the complex rotator will be far more difficult to control. The single rotator was so easy to use; set up, aim, pull the club back to the appropriate angle and let go. Now when we pull the club back on this new machine, we need to worry about the relative rotations of the two pivot points; this machine is kind of rubbery, like a loose skeleton. We can pull the clubface back as before, but who knows what will happen on the forward swing?

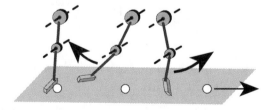

In this figure the lower arm has not kept up with the upper arm.

Tom Purtzer was voted as having the best swing by his fellow PGA members. Does that name ring a bell?

Machine IV: Linear Motion

Finally, consider this machine:

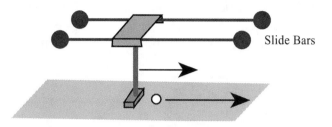

Slide Bars

The clubface is pulled straight back and then pushed forward. There is no rotation, only linear motion. Aiming this machine would be very easy, but finding the right amount of forward push would take considerable practice; it would never be as easy as pulling the club back to a certain angle like we did with the simple rotator.

Machine V: Combination Linear and Rotator

Here is a machine more like the human body.

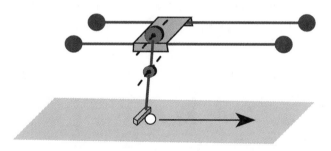

From an engineering standpoint, there is no reason to build a machine like this since the two motions (rotation and linear travel) are redundant. Either form of motion by itself is enough to strike a ball.

From a human standpoint, it is very difficult to do one movement exclusively. Try it for yourself. It is far easier to rotate than it is to move back and forth without any rotation, but it is very difficult to rotate without a slight amount of linear movement.

Machine Vision

We already saw that the simplest position to mount a sighting apparatus would be directly above the target line. Unfortu-

Tommy Armour lost an eye in World War I, but then he won the 1927 US Open, the first of his three major titles.

nately, this is not very practical since people do not view things through a gunsight tube while they are on the golf course.

Suppose we have a robot with a head that contains "eyes" which may pivot inside of sockets, and a "neck" which provides a pivot for the head. We can even add a tongue for that extra balance that some golfers seem to get by sticking it out.

Now the question is how best to position this robot head to see the target line. Obviously we want to find the simplest position that is prone to the least number of errors. It is no surprise that the best place to position the eyes is directly over the target line. Note how the neck and eyes pivot in this figure:

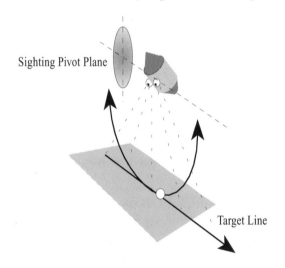

Sighting Pivot Plane

Target Line

It works best when the neck pivots along with the eyes so as to define a vertical "sighting plane." So there is a swing plane, as defined in the previous sections, and there is a sighting plane. If the eyes are placed directly over the target line, the sighting plane must be vertical.

The Art and Science of Putting

Not only is this a machine conclusion, but extensive testing has shown that humans see the target line far better this way as well. You should try it for yourself. A number of golfers see an instant improvement in their accuracy simply by doing this.

Suppose you could bring one single measurement sensor onto the golf course with you. No machines for hitting the ball, only a sensor for measuring such things as slope, speed, wind direction and rain.

1) What would be the most important thing to measure?

2) What would be the least important thing to measure?

3) Would you be a better or worse golfer with the device?

Distance Judgement, or Admiration for Mother Nature

The human brain performs distance calculations in a way so fine and natural that optical engineers marvel at the perfection. Our eyes are slightly separated so that a process of triangulation occurs when relatively close objects are seen. Try closing one of your eyes and judging how far away something is. It is still possible to judge distance with one eye, but it requires a little more time and investigation. Subconsciously the brain is aware of a great many realities, such as gravitational pull (which establishes an intuitive grasp of slope) and sound, which often bears distance information. Our eyes focus and observe the situation, all the while the brain subconsciously extracts and calculates the information we want, such as the distance to a hole. Of course the final answer does not come to us as the precise number of feet or yards. The final answer is an intuitive feel. As inaccurate as this may seem, it works remarkably well. In fact, if you think about it for awhile, it is astounding how well we can do this. Building a machine that could measure the distance

---

Lewis Coleman obtained a patent for ball projecting golf cup. As you can see, the ball is made to pop out of the hole a little while after the putt is made. According to Murphy's law, this device will wait until you look down into the hole to see why it hasn't worked before it shoots the ball right into your eye.

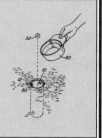

to a hole is not difficult. It could be done with two different sighting tubes separated by a distance and an angle, as shown:

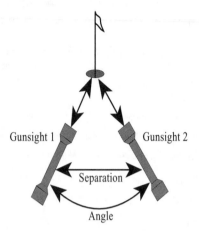

A triangulation process can be done using trigonometry. This is far less admirable than the human process.

But even if we did build a machine that could measure the exact distance to the hole, this single measurement would hardly be enough to base a decision on because the answer would be in terms of feet or yards. Who wants a number? Television announcers usually tell us how long somebody's putt is, but the pro that is attempting the putt does not think in terms of that number.

We need more information, like the wind, the slope and the grain pattern. We could also measure these parameters, but you can see how things would quickly get out of hand. If somebody told you before you were to attempt a putt that the wind speed was North-North-West at 7 knots, the distance to the hole was seventeen feet three inches, blah, blah, blah, you would only be confused.

Suppose now that you had a portable device that kept track of your putting performance. It could record all of your putts so that you could get valuable statistics, such as how often you missed short and right.

1) What would be the most important statistic that you could ask for?

2) What would be the least important statistic that you could ask for?

3) Would you be a better or worse golfer with the device?

The Art and Science of Putting

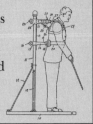

In 1923, Charles Remington obtained this patent. Just strap yourself in and voila! Maybe this could be used while you were sleeping so that when you woke up you could putt like Slammin' Sammy. Does anyone remember if Slammin' Sammy could putt?

Machine Controller

For the machines that were shown above, a controller would include electric motors or some kind of motion initiating device, as well as an electronic circuit, like a computer. We would need to program the timing (tempo), and then we would have to figure out how much force our motion actuators should generate to get the desired motions. We might just add the requirement that the operation be smooth, although this is not strictly necessary.

To control the ramp, all we would need is some kind of gate device that let the ball go from where it was placed on the ramp. This kind of control is very simple, but who cares? This simple machine does not teach anything of value.

For the simple rotator, the controller would pull the rotating arm back to the appropriate angular position and then push it forward. It would not be difficult to program this action. In fact, we do not even need the forward push; all that is really needed is the backward pull and then a "let go."

For the linear motion machine, it would be likewise as simple if we loaded a spring between the slider and the rails. The controller would simply pull the arm back to the appropriate point, and then let go.

Now we run into some severe problems with the double rotator machine. We have two separate joints to consider, and so the world of possibilities expands geometrically over that of a single rotator. Likewise, the errors would expand geometrically so the machine would be extremely difficult to operate with any degree of accuracy.

Technically speaking, a small increase in complexity results in a huge increase in control difficulty. Given a choice between a simple movement and a complex movement, the simple movement can only be better, more accurate and more trustworthy, which is the whole point of the chapter.

On Ben Crenshaw's first golf swing, the ball landed on the green. His teacher said, "Now let's see you knock it into the hole." Ben replied, "Why didn't you tell me that in the first place?" He dropped another ball and proceeded to make an ace on his second ever swing.

A Basic Putting Method

9

Introduction

Putting is entirely personal. Any prescribed method can only be a starting point, and you should ignore anyone that claims to have a method that is anything more. For a method to be a good starting point, it should be very simple. This chapter is the result of the search for the simplest method.

First and Foremost

Putting is comprised of two distinct facets. The first is the decision making and the second is the stroke itself.

The decision making begins well before you get to the putting green. It is much easier to get a general feel for the slope and overall layout of the green from a distance than from directly on top of it. This is especially true for greens with subtle slopes; these are usually impossible to read when you are standing right on them. More often than not, a green that requires the use of a plumb bob simply to tell whether the slope is right or left could have been judged very easily from a distance.

PGA pros usually take their putters from their caddies as soon as they are finished with their approach shot. This helps them get a feel for the club long before they actually use it. It helps them get into the groove. Remember from Chapter 3 that kinesthetic experience (or the sense of touch) is the best way to learn. The quicker you can get a putter into your fingertips, the quicker you will get into the mood for putting.

The culmination of the decision process is an intuitive feel for the green, the weather, the emotional mood, the equipment and the competitive situation. Once the decision has been made, the stroke follows. An experienced golfer knows his stroke, and his decision will be contingent on his strengths and weaknesses.

My first objective in putting has always been to impart topspin to the ball.

Bobby Locke

73

The final decision is nothing more than two things, then. First, the target line is selected, and second, some kind of understanding is reached about how hard to hit the ball. Of course the target line is related to the speed since there is always more than one way to get the ball into the hole.

Once the target line is chosen, it remains to get the ball exactly down that line at the proper speed.

Swing Plane

As was demonstrated in the previous chapters, two things need to happen to make a putt follow the target line:

1) The putter face must be properly oriented with the target line at the point of impact,
2) The putter path must match the target line at the point of impact.

As we saw in chapter 5, the putter face orientation is 85% influential, and the putter path is 15% influential.

These two things are all that really matters. One could do a pirouette on one foot as long as the putter face was square and the putter face was heading down the target line at the point of impact. The best putting stroke, therefore, is the one that will make these two conditions consistent and accurate. Period.

Grip

The normal golf club grip is the overlap, where the pinkie finger on the right hand rests in the groove between the index finger and second finger of the left hand. There is no reason why this grip should be used for putting, and there are very compelling reasons why some other grip should be used. First of all, putting is so much different from the "other" game that a different grip will be a persistent mental reminder. Secondly, there is no need to twist your right hand over your left (another term for this is "release"), as you must do in a full swing. In putting, one of the most deadly sins is to twist your hands while striking the ball.

The most commonly taught putting grip is the "reverse overlap."

The Art and Science of Putting

First place your left hand on the grip, as shown. Leave your index finger loose and put your thumb approximately on top of the shaft. Now place your right hand directly below your left hand as shown. The small finger of the right hand rests directly against the second finger of the left hand (no overlap). All four right hand fingers are wrapped around the shaft. Finally, place your left index finger over your right hand fingertips so that it points down the shaft, toward the putter head. This is called reverse because in the normal golf grip the right pinkie overlaps the left index finger. Now the left index finger does the overlapping.

This may be the most commonly taught method, but it is not necessarily the best one. If you have never used this grip before, you might feel as if you are holding a handful of spaghetti. Furthermore, there does not seem to be any physical reason why this grip should be used. The only motivation seems to be to do something different than the full swing. We want something much simpler than this.

Here is one of the most simple and effective putting grips, the box grip:

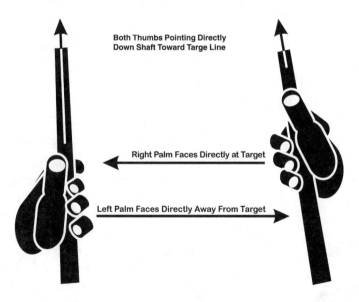

Both Thumbs Pointing Directly Down Shaft Toward Targe Line

Right Palm Faces Directly at Target

Left Palm Faces Directly Away From Target

Place the left hand on the grip with the palm facing directly away from the target and the left thumb pointing directly down the shaft of the club, toward the putter face. Now place the right hand on the grip in inverse fashion, with the palm facing directly toward the target and the thumb pointing directly down the shaft, toward the putter face.

In 1922, Gene Sarazen and Ben Hogan played a special Challenge Match. Sarazen won, but he complained about the butterflies in his stomach. The pain was so intense that he went to see a doctor, who admitted him to emergency surgery. His appendix was removed.

A Basic Putting Method

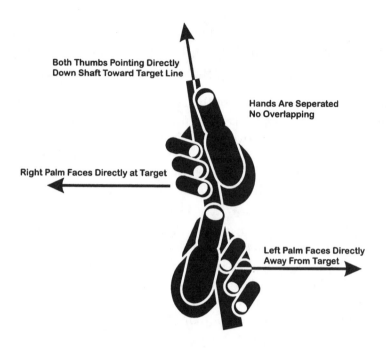

Both Thumbs Pointing Directly Down Shaft Toward Target Line

Hands Are Seperated No Overlapping

Right Palm Faces Directly at Target

Left Palm Faces Directly Away From Target

Do not overlap any of your fingers. In fact, separate your hands as much as you want. Notice that separating your hands "stiffens" the wrist-swinging capability since your wrists no longer comprise a hinge joint.

The geometry of this grip is very clean and there is no strange finger overlap. The human mind likes nicely defined rectangles and this grip makes it easy to visualize the target line. This box grip wins the simplicity award.

A slight deviation of the box grip allows the right index finger to rest on the back of the shaft, pointing down the target line.

Right Index Finger Points at Target Line

This modification seems to give an even better sense of the "box," and an even better sense of the target line since the index finger is now pointing right at it, along with the thumbs. This also suggests a nice clean swing thought; simply imagine your index finger sweeping back and forth over the target line. This is a good focal point for many golfers.

In reality there are as many grips as there are golfers. Pros often change their grips when they are in a rut.

The Art and Science of Putting

From a physical standpoint, the grip is not particularly important; all it needs to do is hold the club firmly. The grip does not swing the club — at least it should not. However, the grip seems to be a key mental indicator, which makes sense because it, along with the feet, is the interface between the golfer and the golf course.

Grip Pressure

It is impossible to describe grip pressure in words. You can grip the death out of the club, or you can hold it gingerly in your fingertips. However, both approaches are open to individual interpretation.

Tour pros all have preferred grips and preferred pressures, but the pressure varies from day to day and from hole to hole. Nervousness and anxiety cause a tighter grip. Tightening is an emotional response, and it is unreasonable to try to dispel emotion from the game. Understanding emotion is far more important and far easier than eliminating it.

The best you can do is to pick up your club and simply study the way you prefer to grip. Study how the tension distributes among the fingers and palms of both hands. It is far more likely that you will be able to vary the distribution than the overall pressure since it more easily definable. Try squeezing from the fingertips and then try squeezing from the palms. The results will be radically different. Try squeezing harder with the left or right hand and see how this affects your stroke.

Some golfers like to grip tightly on short putts as a way of stiffening the wrist movements, and vice versa for longer putts. A lighter grip increases fluidity and feel for speed whereas a firmer grip tends to stiffen the wrists and the lower arms.

Charles Hull obtained a patent for a golfing aid that simply uses two small holes drilled through solid glasses, sort of like the blinders that you put on horses so they are not easily distracted. Supposedly you can see the golf ball through the holes, and therefore all other thoughts and distractions will be eliminated. "Out of sight, out of mind." Out of mind is right.

Like life, golf can be humbling. However, little good comes from brooding about mistakes we've made. The next shot, in golf or in life, is the big one.

Grantland Rice

Setup: Head First

Based on the results of the technical chapters, it is advisable to position the head and eyes directly over the target line. This allows the best visualization of the target line. Based on practical experience, it is also wise to position the head and eyes slightly behind the ball. This allows a better perspective on the target and the overall situation.

Start your stance and setup by placing your head slightly behind the ball, but directly over the target line.

In order to get your head directly over the target line, use whatever posture feels the best for you. Posture does not matter as much in putting as it does in the full swing. Stand upright or bend over; it does not matter. We will get into stances shortly, but for now just do what feels best.

When you move your head to look at the putt (the target line), rotate the neck and eyes as follows:

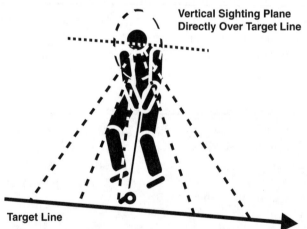

Vertical Sighting Plane
Directly Over Target Line

Target Line

Scan back and forth along the target line on a vertical sighting plane that may be understood as equivalent to a vertical swing plane. This helps visualize the line better so that you can "fix" it into your subconscious. When your eyes are not directly over the target line, a certain amount of subconscious geometry is required to "see" the line. While some people can do this quite well, most people cannot do it at all.

The most compelling reason for keeping your head behind the ball is that it allows a better visualization of the target line as well as the target itself. You are looking forward, toward the intended target; whereas, if your head is in front of the ball, it is more natural to look behind you, away from the target. It is also a good way to make sure that your putter is moving upward very slightly at the point of impact (that is, if your head stays still during the swing). The bottom of the swing arc should be directly below your head, slightly behind the ball.

Stance

The purpose of the stance is to provide a foundation for the swing. No more, no less. The stance should not be involved in the swing, and there should be no shifting of weight during the swing.

For some reason, most beginning golfers feel it is essential to carefully align their feet with the target line. If you try to align your feet with the target line, however, you will probably use your feet as a swing guide to the target line. This induces mental laziness since you should have the target line inscribed within your subconscious as you are swinging. If you do not have a good mental concept of the line, you will not benefit from mechanical devices such as foot placement or the other things that some golfers use. You must strive to "feel" the putt; mechanical contrivance can only suggest and support this feel, not create it.

This figure shows the range of stances:

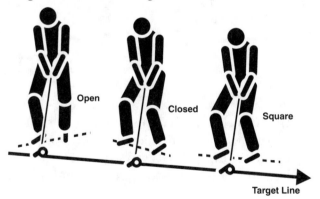

I doubt if anyone ever hits two putts in succession exactly alike.

Walter Hagen

A Basic Putting Method

In the open stance, the left foot is farther away from the target line than the right foot. The left figure shows a closed stance, and the right figure shows a squared stance.

Now the feet may also be open or closed, so this adds another degree of complexity that may be experimented with.

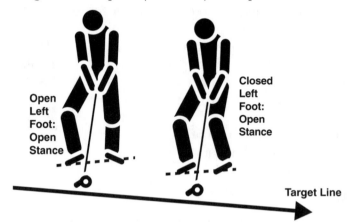

This figure shows only the open stance, with the feet moved around accordingly. The same types of figures could be drawn for a closed stance or a square stance.

The physical effect of opening or closing the stance is usually as follows:

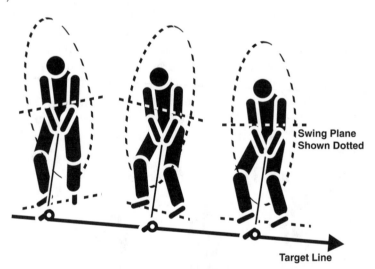

When the stance opens, the swing plane tends to shift open along with the stance. Note that this is not a given fact, it is just an inclination of the human body. You should always adjust your waist to keep the swing plane always parallel with the target line. This means that if you are using the open stance, you should

The Art and Science of Putting

twist your waist so that your shoulders are still square. The goal will always be to keep the shoulders square.

The most common stance is slightly open, with the ball placed closer to the front foot.

This stance often feels better, but that feeling is mental not physical. The reason why this seems better is that it allows you to see the situation. This is why it is called "open." You are open to the situation.

Target Line

On the other hand, many putters tend to pull putts with the open stance, particularly on short putts. This seems intuitive, since it is likely that the shoulders are opened as well as the stance, and therefore the swing plane opens and the clubface is crossing inward at the ball.

Closing the stance or keeping it squared is fine if that is what you want. The swing plane should be defined by the shoulders, not the feet. Opening or closing the stance does not have to mean opening or closing the shoulders. Many putters fall into the trap of moving their stance to move their swing plane.

The balance of weight between the feet is somewhat important, but it should not affect the position of the head; keep it behind the ball. Most professionals favor a slight lean to the left side, toward the target. This does not mean, however, that you have to lean to the left.

Whatever weight distribution you choose should be held constant throughout the putt. Shifting your weight as you do in a full swing tends to pull your head forward and this will destroy the symmetry established with the target line. One of the few universal constants of putting is that it should be done with minimal body movement. If you keep your stance and your head still, the rest will usually fall into place.

Shoulders

Setting up with the shoulders square to the target is the most important element of a simple putting stroke.

The primary goal is to get the swing plane aligned parallel to the target line. The secondary goal is to get the swing plane vertical. Having both at the same time is ideal.

Since the shoulders are such an important component of the swing, they define the swing plane. This means that the

The most popular full swing grip used on the PGA tour is the overlap. The most popular grip used for putting is the reverse overlap. Very few PGA players use the same grip for full swings and putts.

A Basic Putting Method

81

shoulders will be doing most of the swinging while the elbows and wrists and body stay mostly still.

In this figure a putt is shown progressing from the beginning to the follow through. As you can see, the head stays still and behind the ball during the entire swing. The swing plane centered on the middle of the shoulders is shown for visualization purposes. This is how you should attempt to picture the process.

Many good putters line up with their shoulders skewed. Some may be able to make this work, but they are making life more difficult than it needs to be. In order to understand how important square shoulders are to the concept of simplicity, it is necessary to go back to the simple rotator putting machine.

In this figure, the swing plane is square to the target line and vertical:

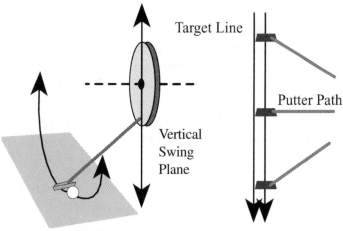

This means that the putter head will stay directly on top of the target line, as shown. As you will recall, this is the simplest way to set up the simple rotator putting machine.

The Art and Science of Putting

We saw that when the swing plane was not parallel to the target line the ball line tended to diverge from the target line.

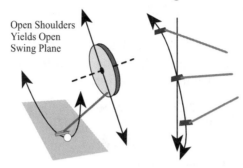

Open Shoulders
Yields Open
Swing Plane

While this may be compensated by opening or closing the clubface at the point of impact, the simplicity rule is clearly violated. The logical and powerful conclusion is that the shoulders should be kept square so that the swing plane can be kept square. If the wrists stay still and do not twist and the shoulder is square, the two conditions for accurate putting are maintained.

Don't worry if you can't make your shoulders perfectly square. Just as it is impossible to truly align your feet with the target line, it is even more difficult to scientifically align your shoulders either square or vertically. In this regard, both concepts are more mental conceptions than physical realities. They are goals, and you should try to imagine them happening as you move your body through the swing process.

It should be noted that assigning the swing plane to the shoulders does not mean that you have to swing exclusively from your shoulders. Your wrists and elbows should move, but just barely. They should simply allow your shoulders to do what they need to do without interfering. The same is true of your waist and your legs and your knees. Be smooth and sweet, but focus your swing at your shoulders.

Hand Position

The best starting point is to let the hands hang directly below the shoulders.

A Basic Putting Method

I would recommend all golfers to model their styles upon the recognized lines that have stood the test of decades of play at the hands of the best amateurs and professionals.

Willie Park

The figure on the left in the previous diagram shows the hands directly below the shoulders, while the figure on the right shows the hands inclined inside, and the right figure shows the hands extended. While it is not physically necessary for the swing plane to incline forward and backward when the hands are not below the shoulders (as is shown by the dotted lines in the figure), it is the most natural response.

Try this for yourself. When you try it, exaggerate the hand placements as much as you can so as to amplify the effect.

Here are several figures showing how the pivot point inclines forward and backward.

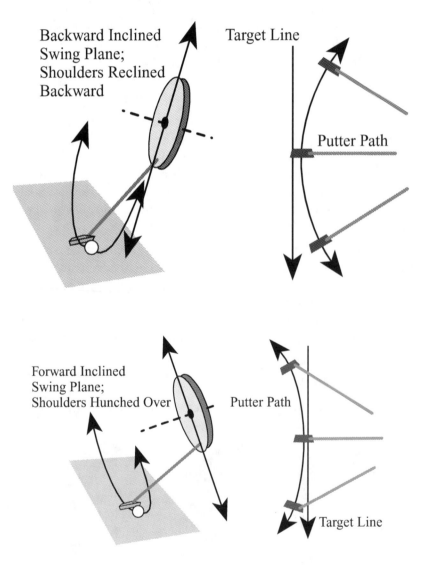

Backward Inclined Swing Plane; Shoulders Reclined Backward

Target Line

Putter Path

Forward Inclined Swing Plane; Shoulders Hunched Over

Putter Path

Target Line

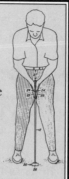

Aaron Sherwood obtained a patent for a golf putter hand grip that you hold between your palms. Supposedly this will help the golfer get a better feel for the target line. As easy as one, two, three. I made one and tried it out. Forget it. I did get a better feel for the target line, but a far stronger feeling was that I was doing something absurd.

Keeping the hands directly below the shoulders is the simplest way to keep the swing plane vertical.

Grip Point

The next question is where to position your hands vertically. The following figure shows the range of positions:

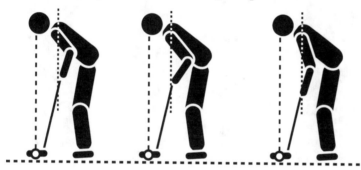

Physics says it does not matter. The swing plane has been nicely established by the square shoulders and by the hands directly below the shoulders.

Most golfers establish their hand positions by virtue of their putter. If they have a long putter, they hold their hands up high. If the putter is short, the hands will go lower.

This brings up an interesting point. Since most golfers select their putter largely by virtue of its feel, they may end up selecting the wrong putter if their stance is incorrect. Then the fact that they have an incorrect putter sustains the problem and prevents the golfer from establishing the right setup. For instance, if you normally stand upright and your head is inside the target line, you probably have a putter that is too long.

You may find, now that you are learning the best way to hold your body and your shoulders, that your putter is not the right length. Obviously if your putter is too long you can easily rem-

A Basic Putting Method

edy this by cutting and regripping. A short putter is another matter. However, do not let your putter dictate your swing.

This is OK

Putter lie is another parameter that might affect the way you want to set up. Do not let lie dictate your setup, though, because the putter face does not have to be lying flat against the green surface

If lie is not quite right, either ignore it or get a putter that has the right lie.

Elbows

The elbows should be comfortable and not eccentric in any way. The range of positions is shown here:

Moving the elbows in and out in relation to the shoulders will cause quite a change in the way you feel. It will not necessarily cause a change in the orientation of the swing plane, unless you are trying to swing from the elbows.

In general, if you hold your elbows tightly against your body (close together), you will be more inclined to swing with your elbows, and this is to be avoided. On the other hand, if your elbows are sticking way out (far away from each other), your swing stiffens up quite a bit and tends to feel unnatural and forced.

In keeping with the simplicity rule, the best bet would seem to be to allow the elbows to suspend below the shoulders in a comfortable and quiet manner. Take them out of the swing.

Try some different combinations of alignment between the shoulders and the elbow positions. Again, be very exaggerated

The Art and Science of Putting

so that you can more readily see the opposing sides of the argument.

Some golfers find that adjusting the elbows helps to prevent skywriting, which is the propensity to move the putter back on a different path than the forward path.

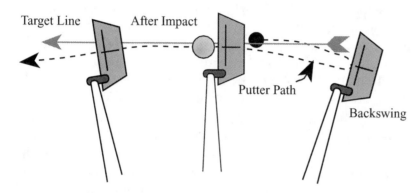

It is far more likely that skywriting is coming from waist twists during the swing than from poor elbow placement. You may want to go back to Chapter 8 and look at the figure of the putting machine that uses both a vertical rotator and a horizontal rotator. The waist originates horizontal rotation very readily. Some lateral movement of the waist toward the target during the forward swing may be desirable (just like the full swing), but rotation is a killer.

Keep the Palms Square to the Target Line

The putter face at impact is critical. If you are using the box grip, you absolutely have to keep your palms square to the target line throughout the swing, particularly at the point of impact. The overwhelming tendency is to twist your right hand over your left, as you are supposed to do in the full swing. This spells death in putting. Keep your wrists square, whatever grip you use.

The Swing

All of the things done to this point are done slowly, deliberately and with calculation. The setup is a physical fact; it can be done precisely like a science. All the body parts are in place, the decision making is finished and the proper attitude has been gained through intuition. Mistakes in setup should be difficult to accept compared to mistakes in the stroke, for you have the time and the deliberation to get the setup right.

You are now ready for the swing.

The one influence most likely to assure the satisfactory progression of the swing is clear visualization in the player's mind of the movement.

Bobby Jones

A Basic Putting Method

One Last Look

You have chosen the target line and the speed by reading the green. You have addressed the ball and taken your stance. Now you take a last look down the target line by swiveling your head on a vertical sitting plane.

Before you strike the ball, you need to relax and "become one" with the target line. While you are actually swinging the putter you need to concentrate on the speed of the putt, so the target line should be inscribed within your subconscious; it should be automatic. You should be able to close your eyes and strike your putt just as straight as if your eyes were opened.

When you are on the practice green, you should pay more attention to whether you are putting straight than whether you are putting for the right distance. As Chapter 3 showed, the purpose of practice is to make certain aspects as automatic as possible. If you can make direction entirely automatic, you will be able to concentrate that much better on the speed of your putt when you are on the golf course.

Remember: the target line is a straight line, and you are hitting down the target line. Many golfers concentrate on the ball line, which is the curved path that you hope your ball will follow. This is wrong! You want to hit your ball down the target line, and it is a straight line. *All putts are straight putts.*

Forward Press

Ben Hogan described the forward press as a running start. Most pros use some form of the forward press for their full swings, and a subtle variation is also useful for putting.

The forward press is really very simple. Just move your hands forward, toward the target, very slightly before you begin your backswing.

The Art and Science of Putting

The left figure shows the hands slightly behind the ball, and the figures progress toward the right. The right-most figure shows the first movement of the backswing.

The forward press should be accomplished without much shoulder movement; it should all be in the wrists and arms. It is mechanically natural for the hands to slightly lead the putter head at that first, initial motion backward. By intentionally moving the hands slightly ahead with the forward press, this non-symmetry is compensated nicely.

Most golfers who have never done this find that after a few practices they adopt the movement wholeheartedly, and it becomes quite natural. From a timing and rhythm standpoint, the forward press forces honesty and flow.

Acceleration Through the Ball

Of all the aspects of the putting stroke, acceleration through the ball is the most important. Ironically, acceleration does nothing of importance from a physics standpoint. The only speed that matters is at the point of impact. It hardly matters whether the club is decelerating or accelerating, as long as the speed at impact is correct. The ball does not know acceleration from deceleration.

But the human body wants an acceleration. Putting is necessarily an active process (for that matter, all sports are). This means that you must go forth with confidence and strike the ball into the hole. If your attitude is one of avoidance of failure, as opposed to an active push for success, your putting will suffer.

It is a natural tendency for golfers to hesitate very slightly at the point of impact. There seems to be a reluctance to "go for it." By accelerating through the ball, you are forced to become more active and assertive.

Most Short Putts Are Missed Because of Pulling

The Skewed Pendulum

Everybody knows how a pendulum swings back and forth, and the concept is excellent for visualizing the tempo of a good putt stroke. A more effective visualization includes a little trick that will radically improve your stroke by forcing you to accelerate through the ball.

A normal pendulum swings back and forth equally, like a metronome.

I believe the first rule for good putting is to take time enough to get settled, compose yourself, make peace with your God and the world, let the universe stop whirling, get the line right, get your grip right, rehearse, relax and shoot right. Don't get muddled.

Don Herold

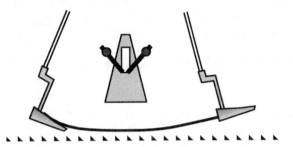

Now, if you pull the putter back a shorter distance than you think you should, you will automatically compensate on your forward swing by moving through the ball more smoothly and with more authority. This may be visualized by the skewed pendulum.

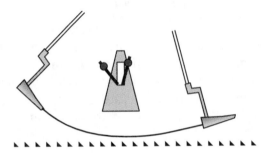

Try pulling the club way back on a short putt (exaggerate) and see how you have a hard time finding the authority and speed that you need at the point of impact.

Now try barely pulling the putter back and see how you are forced to swing through the ball with a far greater authority.

Watch the pros, especially their practice swings. They exaggerate the skewed pendulum in their practice swings. It is an extremely useful and powerful tool.

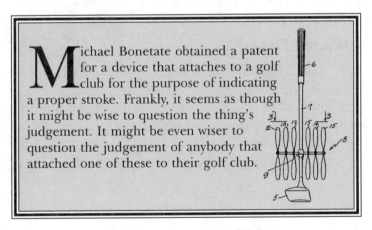

Michael Bonetate obtained a patent for a device that attaches to a golf club for the purpose of indicating a proper stroke. Frankly, it seems as though it might be wise to question the thing's judgement. It might be even wiser to question the judgement of anybody that attached one of these to their golf club.

The Art and Science of Putting

Wrist Release

Another popular and effective device to force authority is to incorporate a very slight wrist release at the point of the impact. This is not the same as for the full swing where the release is done by moving the right hand over the left hand. In the putt release, the wrists stay aligned to the target line, but they simply add a little "touch" to the ball. It is very difficult to describe this motion since it is largely a mental enhancement, not a physical one. It may be viewed as more of a rejection of reluctance than a physical release, a kind of subliminal trigger to be pulled.

If you are using the box grip with the right index finger pointing at the target line, this device becomes even more effective since you can visualize your index finger releasing, instead of your wrists.

Another advantage of the wrist release is that it helps to make sure the clubface is not punching the ball down into the grass.

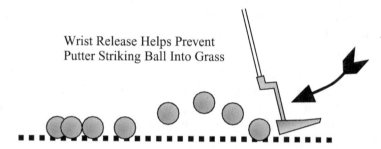

Wrist Release Helps Prevent
Putter Striking Ball Into Grass

Finally, the wrist release can become an excellent focal point for your concentration. If you imagine the tempo and the feel of the putt culminating in that point in time where the wrists actually sweep through the ball, your concentration becomes more focused.

Knee Release

Ben Crenshaw advocates a knee release that works much like the wrist release. Right at the point of impact, move your knees very slightly toward the target. There is no physical justification for this, but it seems to work very well for some golfers. Try it for yourself.

Incidentally, the knee release is also used for chip shots around the green. It helps to pull the club through the ball. In the case of a chip shot, the knee release prevents hitting "fat," or behind the ball. Do not release your knees during putting so

The putting stroke should be as simple as possible.

Billy Casper

much that you end up de-lofting the club at the point of impact by pulling yourself forward, toward the target.

Head Motion

Don't move your head!

There is no good reason, either physical or mental, why the head should move, either back and forth or up and down or in and out. In fact, do not rotate or twist your head either.

On the other hand, trying to keep the head extremely rigid requires concentration, and there are better things on which to concentrate. The point is that head movement should be minimal. If you move your head, look somewhere else for the reason; head movement is a symptom, not a cause.

Concentrate on Distance When Putting

Once the target line is decided, hitting down that line should be automatic. The mind should be concentrating on the distance during the actual putting activity. The target line may be defined and relatively well articulated, while the speed can only be understood by a sense of what it should be; this is impossible to define.

Note the term used is distance, not speed. You want to putt for distance, not speed. Of course you will need the right speed to make a putt go a certain distance, but it is the distance that you are after. This is a question of mental semantics, but subtleties like this will elevate your game.

Remember: *All putts are straight putts.* Get the curves out of your mind when you are hitting the ball.

Pattern

Both the human mind and the human body crave pattern, or habit. A consistent, definable, simple method that is always approached identically will increase your putting effectiveness. Always go through the same preparations, the same way, and in the same order.

Here is a suggested order that you may want to change around for your own personal preferences.

1) Inspect your putt from in front and in back, and then from the sides. Walk down the putt line, (off to the side a couple of feet or so).

2) Go several feet behind your ball and choose the line. This usually takes the form of deciding how many inches left or right of the hole to aim for.

The Art and Science of Putting

W atch the pros on television and answer the following:

1) What is their stance?

2) Where are their hands?

3) Where are their shoulders?

4) What is their overall tempo?

5) How far back do they bring the club?

6) Do they keep their head still?

7) What is their head position?

8) What is their pattern? (To answer this question, you will
have to watch for several holes. You will probably see the
same pattern on each hole.)

9) Do they take their putter from their caddie as soon as
they can?

10) Do they putt with a glove?

3) Visualize your mental target line; feel comfortable with
it.

4) Stand to the side of the ball and take several practice
swings with the distance and rhythm of your putt. Use
the skewed pendulum swing but exaggerate the skewed
motion. Feel the target line when you are taking your
practice swings. Visualize the ball going down the
target line (not the ball line).

5) Address the ball; take your stance and do it very me-
thodically.

6) Concentrate on the line until you feel comfortable with
it. Eliminate numbers, technicalities and complexity in
your thought process.

7) Take a few easy breaths, relax. Smile to yourself now, in
honor of being on a golf course on such a fine day.
After all, the worst day golfing is far better than the
best day working. Remember, once the ball leaves your
clubface, a lot of random influences are going to start
in, so it is counterproductive to try too hard.

8) Concentrate on the distance of the putt, and then
stroke the ball with authority and activity.

Reading the green should be a little more free form, determined by the conditions, but the putt itself should be very pat-
terned. Anything that can be made automatic will help you to

*Eighty percent
of all golfers
never finish the
backswing
before the
downswing is
under way.*

**Grantland
Rice**

A Basic Putting Method

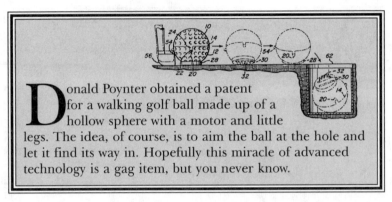

Donald Poynter obtained a patent for a walking golf ball made up of a hollow sphere with a motor and little legs. The idea, of course, is to aim the ball at the hole and let it find its way in. Hopefully this miracle of advanced technology is a gag item, but you never know.

concentrate on your swing thought. You can only concentrate on one thing.

Watch the pros and you will see many different patterns, but each pro has one. Many pros try to align the face of the putter prior to anything else. They set it down in front of the ball, then behind the ball, and then align their stance and body accordingly. There is no good reason for doing this other than pattern.

Have Fun

Golf is a game. I repeat myself, but this is too important a point. If you lighten up before you hit each putt, you will putt much better. This is fact, pure and simple, and there is no arguing allowed. The irony is rich. If you want to do better, stop trying so hard and you will. Surely this is a generalization that applies to many more things than putting.

The Great Putters and Their Styles

Bobby Locke put both his thumbs down the center of the shaft. He gripped very lightly with his fingers and never changed his putting grip from one putt to the next.

His feet were placed four inches apart with the left foot three inches ahead of the right in a closed stance and the weight evenly distributed. The ball was placed opposite the left toe. When he addressed the ball, he placed the toe of the putter directly behind the ball, and then on his forward swing he corrected this offset and hit the ball on the sweet spot. This is hardly recommended but how can one say not to do it when Bobby Locke won so many tournaments doing it?

His takeaway went inside with no wrist action and the putter face stayed square to the hole all the way through the swing, so his pivot plane was vertical. His follow through equaled his backswing, so he used a symmetric pendulum style stroke.

Let's face it, 95 percent of this game is mental. A guy plays lousy golf, he doesn't need a pro, he needs a shrink.

Tom Murphy

The Art and Science of Putting

Billy Casper tried to "feel" the putt with the right thumb and index finger. He used a reverse overlap grip with an easy but firm grip pressure, whatever that means. He distributed his weight equally and he varied his stance according to the situation. He used his wrists quite liberally, forcing the putter head to go upward quite a bit on the backswing, and therefore dipping at the ball on the forward swing. On shorter putts he used even more wrist to enhance the feel.

He was very quick and deliberate and positive. Billy had an excellent outlook on life, feeling that his family was far more important than the game. This was perhaps his greatest strength. Golf was nothing more than a game for him.

Gary Player never putts with a glove and he uses an overlap grip with his left index finger pointing toward the ground and his hands very close together. He positions his eyes meticulously over the ball and his weight over his left heel and he stands very close to the ball, thereby requiring a very upright putter.

On shorter putts, Gary "taps" the ball. On longer putts he sweeps the ball. He always keeps his body absolutely still and his head down well after the ball is on its way. He pulls the clubface slightly inside on the backswing.

Jack Nicklaus uses a reverse overlap grip with firm fingers and the right palm parallel to the face of the club (palm is facing directly toward the hole). He considers his right forefinger important for a sense of touch. These are all things that are recommended.

He does not consider stance or posture very important, and he will vary. His eyes are directly over the target line and he likes to keep the putter shaft vertical. The position of the ball is off his left toe, and he likes to look forward toward the hole when he putts.

His tempo is very leisurely and patient, just like everything he does on the golf course. He takes his time reading and absorbing the situation. He likes the swing thought of the ball "dying" into the hole (as opposed to Arnold Palmer's charging the hole). He spends a long time crouching over the ball in order to get the right "feel," not the right mechanics. Jack is a believer in intuition.

Arnold Palmer uses a reverse overlap grip with light pressure and good control. His right hand is the major controlling factor, and he likes to feel the putt with his right hand. Early on, Arnold kept his knees inward, with pigeon-toed feet to keep his

When you reflect on the combination of characteristics that golf demands of those who would presume to play it, it is not surprising that golf has never had a truly great player who was not also a person of extraordinary character.

Frank Tatum, Jr.

body from moving. His eyes were directly over the ball at all times.

His most important aspect was to keep very still and not move his body. He charged at the hole; a firm believer in the maxim, "never up, never in." On his backswing, his clubface closed and after impact it opened. This is very distinctive and not recommended. He did this by using a lot of wrist action. This is definitely not recommended.

Ben Crenshaw uses a reverse overlap grip with the thumbs on top of the shaft for better feel. His palms face each other in the box grip style. His eyes are parked slightly inside the target line, and his upper back curves toward the horizontal. His hands are kept directly below his shoulders and his stance is almost square and slightly open with his feet six inches apart.

He uses a definite arm and shoulder stroke with the wrists very solid throughout. Ben is probably the best putter to not use his wrists, except in the long putts. A steady head is one of his absolutes. His tempo is very patient and rhythmic, like a nice, slow pendulum. He seldom, if ever, allows his left wrist to break.

One of Ben's secrets is to allow his knees to break very slightly toward the target right at the point of impact. This is something like the wrist release advocated in this book. It is more psychological than mechanical.

When all is said and done, and whatever the method and whoever the man, successful putting surely must be a matter more of nerve than technique.

Pat Ward-Thomas

The Art and Science of Putting

Tips and Helpful Items

10

Some Random Tips for the Green

Mozart

An interesting experiment showed that students who listen to Mozart prior to taking mathematics tests score higher on their tests. Why? Rhythm and pattern are described in terms of mathematics. Music is a form of mathematics, as odd as that may sound. The reason that music is pleasing to the human conscience is due to its rhythm and pattern. So, if you listen to music while you putt, will you putt better?

Well, yes.

Although you would do well to remember that all music is not created equal. For instance, if you listen to rock and roll while you are practicing, it is likely that you will jab aggressively at the ball. Mozart, on the other hand, is very soothing and smooth. As mood music, Mozart elicits peace and tranquillity. Mozart was a genius in terms of harmonizing with the natural human response to friendly patterns.

Try using a Sony Walk-Man or other such system and listen to Mozart during your practice. If Mozart isn't your style, try something else which you feel is flowing and smooth. Music is as subjective as anything else in this book.

Every Putt is a Straight Putt

This is because you putt every one straight down the target line. Too many golfers try to visualize the ball path.

And many golfers fall into the bottomless pit of attempting to put some kind of English on the ball because of break and conditions. They try to "curve" the ball like bowlers do; in fact, many golfers do this subconsciously, so you might be doing it

The fixity of a habit is generally in direct proportion to its absurdity.

Proust

Theodore Schmidt obtained a patent for a croquet style golf putter. The only real advance in the state of the art here is the flats that are on the grip. Supposedly this style of putter will be easier to aim and hit with. He further claims that a relatively short shaft and handle will give better control. Putters are not really short, and in fact, a lot of golfers prefer long putters, so this claim is doubtful. Try it for yourself. Grip your putter way down, right on the metal shaft, and see how it feels. Why there seems to be such an attraction to croquet style putters is unknown.

without even knowing it. Think of every putt as a straight putt, right down the target line.

Speed Before Break

As discussed in Chapter 4, the speed of a green and the amount of break to play are closely related. You must never forget that to read the break of a green, you must first read the speed. Always in that order. The break of a green is a result of both the speed and the slope.

Watch Your Approach Roll

This should be obvious, but it is surprising how many golfers fail to use this information. When you chip or hit a long putt, you can generally see some slope, and you can certainly read some speed. Pay attention; most golfers tend to hit their ball and then stare as though they are dispassionately watching television. Ask yourself, "Did that shot roll as I thought it would? Why not?" In particular, if your approach rolls past the hole, you can preview what your putt will be like. It is amazing how many golfers fail to use this information.

Ball Past Hole

Never Up, Never In. This philosophy has another advantage that is largely ignored. When you hit your putt past the hole, you can see the way the ball breaks as it travels past the hole. This is the approximate line you want to find on the way back, so you have given yourself a preview. Obviously if you leave your ball short, you do not enjoy this free information. This is another reason to hit aggressively and actively at the hole. Many golfers turn away in disgust or frustration when they miss.

Stat Sheets: Keep a Record

One of the best ways to improve your putting effectiveness is to keep a record. There are many ways to do this, but the only important thing is to be consistent.

The following method works very well.

1) Make copies of a grid, or use grid paper. Try to make the grid so that a quarter of an inch of paper is equal to a foot of green. An average green will easily fit onto a sheet of paper. If you want to save paper, just draw in the end of the putt, not the beginning, and note how far the putt was.

2) The direction (North, South, East or West) is irrelevant, although it may be used if you wish. Indicate the break somehow, for instance an arrow. The break changes over the course of a few yards, so your drawing will be only an approximation, but that will be good enough.

3) For the first putt, draw a line representing the ball line.

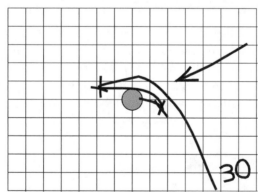

If your putt was too long to fit onto the page, indicate this somehow.

The detail you need is the approximate break and whether you missed left, right or long or short. The figure shown indicates a three putt from 30 feet, with the first putt breaking to the left, the second putt missing to the left (pulled) and the third putt going in.

4) After the round, look over your record and try to find patterns.

Tips and Helpful Items

Winners know from experience how they will react to the excitement and pressure of a final-round shoot-out. They find a way to perform even when their legs and arms go rubbery and their heartbeats make the logos on their shirt jump up and down.

Peter Jacobson

It is very common for a bad habit to show itself after eighteen holes of golf. For instance, if you miss thirteen holes on the low side of the hole, you are obviously under-reading. Probably the most common error for amateurs is to under-read putts (miss on the low side of the hole). You can learn a lot by tracking your performance.

Line Versus Point Putting

The target line may be visualized several ways. The two most common are the line and the point methods.

In the line method, the golfer visualizes an actual straight line going along the grass. This would be much like drawing a chalk line right where you want the ball to travel. Obviously you cannot draw a line, so the question is how to visualize most effectively.

In the point method, a single point is visualized somewhere a few feet down the target line. The ball is then "rolled" over this point.

The choice is dictated solely by preference. Some people can visualize lines very effectively, while some visualize points better. Most golfers have never really stopped to consider exactly how they visualize, so experimenting and establishing either method will be an improvement.

Consider using the point method for shorter putting and the line method for longer putts. When a putt is very short, most golfers picture the hole itself as a target. But the hole is a relatively wide target when up close. Picture a point in front of the hole over which you want your ball to pass. Your precision will increase.

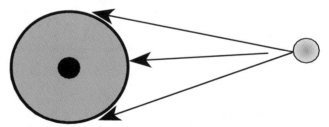

Aim for the Center of the Hole, Not the Hole

Hit Versus Swing

Although the net result will be the same, the mental concept of hitting the ball versus swinging through the ball are far different ways of playing the game.

The Art and Science of Putting

Swinging through the ball will cause a better follow through, and in particular a better acceleration through the ball. Especially as the concept of "hitting" suggests that the end of the act is obtained when the ball is hit. This is clearly not the case if you are accelerating through the ball, a continuous action.

Imparting Forward Spin

Some of the best putters of all time have intentionally attempted to impart forward spin on the ball by using the wrists to "release" upward at the point of impact.

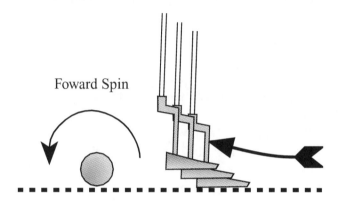

Foward Spin

This is more of a mental advantage than a physical one since the physics of ball contact say that forward spin is nearly impossible to achieve. Of course the ball will start spinning on its own by coming in contact with the grass.

Push Versus Pull

Somewhat related to the hit versus swing concept is the push versus pull. Are you pushing the clubhead through the ball, or are you pulling it through the ball? This is related to the concept of grip pressure and grip control. If you are right-handed and your right hand is dominant, you are probably a pusher. If the left prevails, you are probably a puller.

Sink the Putter Instead of the Ball

On short putts it is often useful to imagine the putter head being pushed straight at the hole, instead of imagining the ball rolling at the hole. This will help you follow through and avoid "hitting" the ball or pulling the ball to the left.

Head Steady

One of the most common reasons for missing putts is a slight head nod toward the hole right at the point of impact.

When you miss a shot, never think of what you did wrong. Come up to the next shot thinking of what you must do right. The average expert player hits six, eight or ten real good shots a round. The rest are good misses.

Tommy Armour

Tips and Helpful Items

Of course, thinking about keeping your head motionless violates the rule that you must perform positive activity, not avoid negative activity. It is better to try to think about what to do instead of what not to do, so visualize your stationary body in conjunction with an active shoulder swing. Only one thought.

Putting From the Fringe

You will often want to putt a ball that is on the fringe close to the green. Before you actually do this, there are several things worth noting:

1) It is very easy to hit the grass before the ball, resulting in disaster. You must keep the club above the grasslevel. This often means hitting near the bottom of the putter and near the top of the ball.

   The laws of physics state that this will put a downward force on the ball at impact. Beware of jamming the ball into the grass; this will destroy the putt as sure as the sun shines.

2) If the lie is poor, there is a good chance that putting will jab the ball into the grass and therefore result in a short putt. Use a wedge.

3) It is good to try to "lift" the ball out of the grass by intentionally hitting upwards on it. This is like trying to impart a forward spin on the ball, but in an exaggerated sense. It helps to put the ball forward in the stance.

4) Sometimes the ball is very slightly kicked to the side when it steps from the fringe, down onto the green surface.

   The steeper the approach angle, the worse the problem; the larger the difference in grass lengths, the worse the problem. The only real remedy is to try to

The person who enjoys his work as much as he does his hobby is a genius. The golfer who lets frustration destroy the pleasure of the game is a fool.

anonymous

The Art and Science of Putting

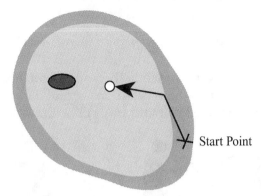

Start Point

predict this and compensate accordingly. Good luck.

5) In general, the problem is usually one of predicting the right speed to hit through the fringe. This is complicated because there are two speeds: that of the fringe and the green surface. Both must be read correctly.

Fringe clearly is slower than green, so the putt needs to be hit harder than if the putt were all green. Almost all putts attempted from the fringe end up short; check yourself to see if this is true. You might have some success in equating one foot of fringe with several feet of green. In other words, if there is three feet of fringe, consider this to be the same as seven feet of green. In order to do this adequately, you will have to practice.

Long Putter

The long putters are relatively new to the game of golf, and there is not much established wisdom. Some players use their chin to anchor the end and some use their bodies in the swing. It may be true that golfers that use the long putters favor individuality more than most (which is why they are using the club in the first place).

Normal procedure seems to be:

1) Hold the top of the club as you would hold a microphone, with your left elbow out.

2) Grip about two feet lower with your right hand, keeping your palm down the target line.

3) Pull your left hand against your chest.

4) Try to get your eyes over the target line.

When all is said and done, and whatever the method and whoever the man, successful putting surely must be a matter more of nerve than technique.

Pat Ward-Thomas

Other than that, try to get a nice square shoulder turn and try to keep the swing plane vertical.

Throwing a Putter Into the Lake

First of all, be careful. While throwing a club is very gratifying, it might turn out to be very expensive and dangerous. Make sure to keep your head still and you will be far more accurate.

The Most Common Problems

The Yips

The yips are a psychological problem related to anxiety, and the only way to cure the yips is to cool down and remember that golf is only a game. Of course this is easy to say, but it is the only way to really tackle the problem. Simply understanding that there is a maximum performance level that you are capable of will help you understand that short of perfection is the norm, not something to fear.

Short or Long Backswing

Many golfers have poor tempo, or rhythm. The most common problem is to pull the putter away from the ball too quickly and too far back. This results in a deceleration at the ball, and a twisting motion in the swing.

Many golfers also tend to begin their forward swings before they are finished with the backswing. This results in both bad tempo and bad loft at the point of impact.

You may find that pulling the putter away too quickly kinks your shoulders out of alignment simply because the shoulders are saddled with the burden of moving the club quickly. The shoulders have the biggest muscles, and so they are called upon to do the heavy work. Even if you have decided that you are a wrist putter, your shoulders are going to flinch if you try to move too quickly.

In golf, as in no other sport, your principal opponent is yourself.

Herbert Warren Wind

The Art and Science of Putting

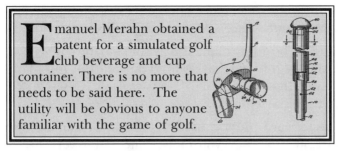

Emanuel Merahn obtained a patent for a simulated golf club beverage and cup container. There is no more that needs to be said here. The utility will be obvious to anyone familiar with the game of golf.

The remedy is to practice the skewed pendulum where the backswing is very short and smooth. Visualize a skewed pendulum as you swing. And practice patience; the lack thereof may be the root of the problem.

Sky-Writing

Sky-writing is a term used to describe the problem of bringing the club back on one line, then circling around inadvertently and bringing it back to the ball on another line. The term is generally used with regard to the full swing, but it also applies to putting.

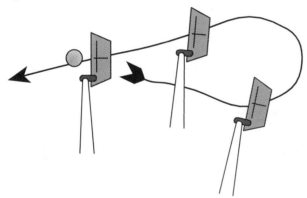

It should be evident that sky-writing makes good, square contact very difficult. It should also be evident that it would cause no serious damage to the shot if the club-face is square at impact. However, it is extremely difficult to make the clubface square when you and the putter are doing the loop-de-loop. Square becomes a question of tempo and there are enough problems in putting without inviting this one.

Try to square the shoulders and elbows to the target line. This problem can also occur due to moving the head and body.

Another source of the problem may be that your elbows are moving in and out as you swing. You need to hold still throughout the entire swing.

The person I fear most in the last two rounds is myself.

Tom Watson

Try moving your stance open or closed, and your shoulders along with your stance and see if this will solve the problem.

You may be guilty of pressing your club into the grass so that when you begin your backswing you pull the top of the club back faster than the clubface. Sky-writing is then an effort to right this initial wrong.

The forward press is used to "break the static inertia." A forward press is when you move your hands very slightly forward, toward the target, just prior to your swing. It is a kind of running start. It may help you avoid sky-writing in your putting since it is apparently very difficult for many golfers to start their swing process smoothly.

The initiation of the swing seems to cause more problems than any other facet. This is probably due to the same human effect that makes short putts so difficult. The human body wants a certain minimum amount of movement before the sense of rhythm can kick in. Many things we do very well at full speed are nearly impossible to duplicate in slow motion.

Starting your forward swing with shoulder twist (baseball habit) will result in the clubface coming from outside to in, or "pulling" as it is called in the full swing. Baseball habits are responsible for a lot of poor golf.

Clubface Not Aligned with Target Line

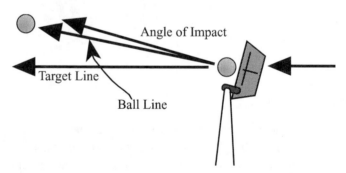

This is simply a problem of perception. For whatever reason, some people have a difficult time visualizing the clubface perpendicular to the target line. There are laser pointer devices available that help considerably with this problem, but they are not cheap and they cannot be used on the golf course.

Consistent practice will teach the proper alignment. It should be noted that even though some people have a difficult time visualizing perpendicularly, they are normally consistent in their

The Art and Science of Putting

errors. This suggests that the problem is not random slop, but one of visualization. There is an important distinction between the two, and the first step toward solving the problem is to understand of which one you are guilty. Keeping a record will help.

Twisting Clubface at Impact

The full swing requires a wrist twist. Do this on a putt and it spells death.

Put your right hand with the palm facing the target, your left with the palm facing directly away from the target and keep both in that orientation throughout the putt. Accelerate through the ball and keep your head still throughout the swing. A particularly good device is to extend your index finger so that it is pointing at the target line throughout the swing, especially during the follow-through.

Many golfers jab at the ball without following through. Try this and you will see the twist happen. This is especially true on short putts, where the most common reason for missing is pulling.

Bad Loft (Hitting into the Grass)

Putter Striking Ball Into Grass

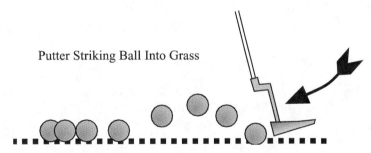

This is caused by improper tempo, or by moving your head through the putt. Keep your head behind the ball all the way through the swing, particularly at impact. In fact, keep your head still, period. Try moving your hands very gently upward as you go through the ball. If you bring the club backwards with a shoulder movement, and then sweep linearly forward with your upper body, the putter face will be aiming downward at impact.

This may also be an equipment problem related to the loft of the putter. The most natural solution for your needs may be to find a putter with the proper loft.

Undecided Line

Many golfers are still calculating the line as they stand over the putt. You should choose the line before you address the ball. You should address the ball based on the line — that is how you first set up your stance, and then how you align your clubface. If you are still trying to read the line of the putt as you are standing over the putt, you are guilty of mental laziness. Do your work in the right order, with the right pattern.

Different Speeds with One Putt Style

Beginners may want to use a single putting style, but as you get better you should be able to improvise, just as you do with a full swing.

You may want to try different stances and body alignments for right breaking versus left breaking putts. It seems natural for many golfers to use a closed stance when the ball is breaking left, and an open stance when the ball is breaking right.

Different styles are also applicable to different speeds. Your feet may be further apart for longer putts. Your grip may be different, hand separation in particular.

It is far more natural for the human body to accelerate through the ball when putting a further distance, so your mental attitude may be shifted. You do not need to try to accelerate

James Dale obtained a patent for a golf putting practice device that is basically little more than a wheel. He claims that it will help a golfer determine the exact striking "attitude" of the golf club at the point of impact. Apparently, if you hit the wheel with a skewed putter face, it will magnify the error, so you can use this to help you analyze your putter face angle at impact. The problem, of course, is aligning it with the intended target line. If your alignment is one degree off, but your putt stroke is perfect, it will tell you that you are one degree off. There is no good way to align such a small device to an accuracy anywhere near one degree.

The Art and Science of Putting

so much with longer putts; your body will automatically do this. You can concentrate more on the speed of a long putt.

Most three putts are not a result of incorrect reading or alignment, but incorrect distance. For longer putts, your priorities might change to addressing speed more than line.

Common Equipment Problems

1) Too much or too little loft.

2) A wrong lie will encourage a more upright or less upright stance than you might like. This is not as important as it is with a full swing, but it may be causing problems nevertheless, particularly if it is forcing you into a stance that you find unnatural. Keep in mind that you want your head directly over the putt line. Some putters are too long for this to be practical; you have to bend your elbows too much, up into your chest. Some putters are so short that the golfer must bend too far over the target line.

3) The weight of the putter may be out of character for you. The weight of the head versus the weight of the shaft determines the tempo. There is a very wide range of putters when it comes to the moment of inertia (determined by both the weight of the head and the length). Have you ever tried a wooden putter?

4) Try putting without a glove. Most professionals do, and there is certainly no reason to wear one while putting. A glove keeps your hand from being torn up by the force of a full swing. Perhaps removing your glove during putting will increase your mental effectiveness.

5) Most putters have some kind of alignment registration marks. These registrations should have two functions. First, they should allow the golfer to visualize the clubface so that it will be easy to align the club with the target line. Each golfer visualizes in his or her own way. It is likely that you will feel more comfortable with certain registrations. Second, they should indicate the sweet spot.

6) Grips often have registrations of their own, usually a flat spot directly away from your body. There is no reason why this flat cannot be moved around, for instance to the back of the club (directly away from the

Anyone who criticizes a golf course is like a person invited to a house for dinner who, on leaving, tells the host that the food was lousy.

Gary Player

target) where you may like to place the palm of your right hand.

And it could be that the flat is distracting, in which case you may want to simply use a normal grip. You can make the grip thicker or thinner, longer or shorter to suit. There are some grips on the market that actually have contours where your fingers should go. This is fine if your personal preference says that these contours are where your want your fingers, but the likelihood is that the contours are simply going to force you to conform in a way that is not natural for you. And these grips are illegal, which may or may not be a problem for you.

Exercises and
Practice

11

Green Slope Reading

You can practice reading the slope of a green by simply bringing along a level the next time you go out. First try to read with your eyes, then put the level in place. You can also use a ramp (see Chapter 4) and point it into different directions.

Use a Ramp to Roll Ball in Four Directions

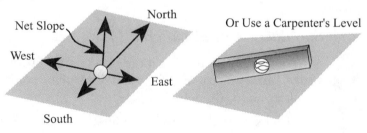

Putting With a Long Putter

Try to find a long putter and work with it for awhile. Note the difference in tempo and study the difference in the pivot point. This will force you to consider the pivot plane and the pivot point. The long putter will help remove your wrists from the swing since the long putters require mostly shoulder pivot and elbow movement, not to mention some hip vinegar.

You have to make corrections in your game a little bit at a time. It's like taking your medicine. A few aspirins will probably cure what ails you, but the whole bottle might just kill you.

Harvey Penick

Putting with Heavy Gloves

Try putting with heavy gloves on your hands. It is amazing how different the entire process feels. This exercise forces you to "tune into" the putter better since you cannot feel it very well. You must try harder to feel the balance and weight. Combine this with closing your eyes and you will take the exercise a step further.

Putting Between Two Objects

Set up two golf clubs, as shown.

Putt between these guides, watching to make sure you do not go too far inside or outside. A golfer is often surprised to learn just how far he is moving the clubhead off the target line. The point is not to eliminate the movement, but to understand it. Chapter 8 discusses machines and the causes and effects of inside to outside movement, as well as outside to inside movement.

Shoulders Moved Differently

Try to keep your left shoulder very still during your stroke. Also try to keep it low. Try to pivot your right shoulder about the left shoulder.

This exercise develops an understanding of the swing plane.

Putt With One Arm Only

Simply grip your putter with your left hand only and take some swings. You can also do this with your right hand.

This exercise will make you develop your grip all the way through the swing. It is a common problem for a golfer to pull the putter back with the left hand and then let the right hand take over and push the putter back through the ball. While this is not strictly taboo, good left arm control is usually better.

Use a Sweatband

If you like a firm wrist swing, try slipping a sweatband or other similar elastic over the wrist and the shaft of the grip.

This forces you to develop the motion of keeping your wrists still and controlling the swing with your shoulders and left wrist. Keep in mind that you may or may not want to do this. A small amount of wrist release is highly desirable, so this exercise will make you sensitive to the position and movement of your wrists. You may just want to use this exercise to show you how wrist movement is related to a good swing.

Putt to a Tee Instead of a Hole

Putting at a point instead of a hole will force you to concentrate on your line with more focus. A hole has width. The closer you are to the hole, the more width it will appear to have. In general, you should try to concentrate on a line (or a point) instead of a width. This is usually not a problem until you get closer to the hole.

Putting With Closed Eyes

Try putting with your eyes closed. Set up, align and get ready as you always do, but right before you start your swing, close

Hugh McTeague obtained a patent for a mechanical putter that allows a golfer to "repeat a selected arc of the club as many times as is necessary for him to learn the effect of the clubhead on the ball for that arc of motion." He then goes on to say that this will teach a golfer how far back to take the putter. This is the same thing as the simple rotator machine presented in chapter eight.

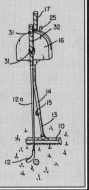

Troubles are like babies — they only grow by nursing.

Douglas Jerrold

your eyes. This promotes better overall concentration and an enhanced visualization of the entire putting process. It also increases your balance and perception.

No Peeking: Predicting Where A Putt Will Go

After you have hit the ball, look at the spot the ball was hit from; do not look up at the putt. Now try to predict where your putt is going to end up before you look up to see where it has actually gone. If you feel you hit exactly how you wanted, and you still made a poor putt, then you are guilty of a mental error or a decision error.

This is an excellent exercise in a more general sense. Of all the exercises, this one has the best potential to make you a better golfer because it forces you to "feel" your putting. This exercise is also very powerful since it forces you to make a distinction between mental errors and physical errors. Most amateurs do not bother to make this important distinction.

Use Lead Tape

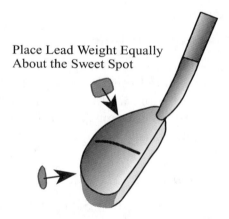

Place Lead Weight Equally About the Sweet Spot

You can obtain lead tape from golf shops. It is used to weigh the clubhead differently. Try adding some to the bottom or the back of your putter and see how it feels.

Extra weight changes the physics of the swing process quite dramatically. It may help you to slow down your tempo since it is more difficult to swing a heavier club. It may also help you follow through better.

Adding lead tape to the back of the putter increases the breadth of the sweet spot. If you add most of the tape directly to the back of the sweet spot, this is not true. Try putting the weight equally on opposite extremes of the sweet spot.

The teacher experiences no grave difficulty in having a student understand the importance of putting. Getting them to practice it is quite another matter.

John Duncan Dunn

Using a Length of String

This exercise may take some time to perfect, but it is advantageous for those who have a difficult time visualizing the curvature of a ball on a sloped surface. Chapter Four described the action of a golf ball as it rolls along a slope, but sometimes it is difficult to draw a bridge between a theory presented on paper and the reality of a golf green.

Take a length of string and place it down on the green along the line you think your putt will travel.

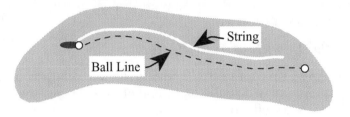

Then hit a ball several inches to the side of the string and observe. Readjust the string and hit again. Study the curvature of the string, and in particular note how the final configuration of the string differs from your original assessment. You can repeat this exercise on different greens. Over time you will notice that your reading is becoming far more accurate.

How much do you think you need to practice and play to get to a ten handicap? How about a five? How about scratch?

How much do you practice putting versus the full swing?

How do you concentrate when you practice? What do you work on as far as concentration when you practice?

Putt a Number of Balls Along the String

Once you have accurately placed a string onto the green, as in the exercise above, place a number of golf balls at intervals along the string, as shown. Hit the closest one to the hole, then move outward.

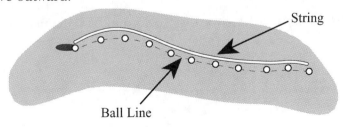

I don't think I've ever gotten scared on the golf course. After all, what is there to be afraid of? I'm not going to die or lose my family, not even all my money. It's first a game.

Ray Floyd

This exercise will develop your ability to picture the break line as well as to get a feel for hitting the ball a certain distance along the break line. In particular, it will help you realize that reading the roll path of a ball begins at the hole, not at the ball.

Putt With Both Feet Together

This exercise will force you to use your upper body exclusively. This will likewise force you to improve your tempo since the most common reason for a stabbing, quick forward swing is that the legs pull forward. If you pull forward with your feet planted directly together, you will probably lose your balance.

Vary the Length of Your Putter

You can grip your putter further down the shaft, even below the grip. You may actually like the feel of a shorter shaft. It is very easy to saw off a putter and put the grip back on if you like a shorter putter (although the opposite is not true).

This has the inverse effect of placing lead tape on the clubhead; it is easier to swing the putter when it is shorter. Perhaps a shorter putter with lead tape will yield better results.

> **P**ay attention to line more than distance when you practice. You want to make the line automatic; you can never make the distance, or speed, automatic.

Stop Your Putter at Rear of Swing

When your putter is at the rearmost part of the swing, stop it for a few moments before swinging forward. This exercise promotes better tempo and rhythm. It is a common mistake for a golfer to begin his forward swing before his back swing is finished, particularly when agitated or nervous. Stopping the swing between back and fore will prevent this. If you find yourself particularly nervous on the golf course, try doing this for your practice putts before you actually hit the ball. It may work wonders.

Surround the Hole

Set up balls at the same distance from the hole, in all directions.

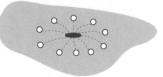

The Art and Science of Putting

First try three feet, then go to four, etc. This is a particularly good exercise to do on a sloped surface because it develops an excellent feel for break.

In this exercise, try to putt the ball so that it always stops an equal distance past the hole (if you miss the putt, that is). You might also try moving about the circumference in different ways. For instance, first move from ball to ball, all the way around the hole. Then move back and forth, back and forth.

Lagging to a Large Diameter Hole

Sometimes it is a good idea to visualize a large diameter hole when lagging for a putt.

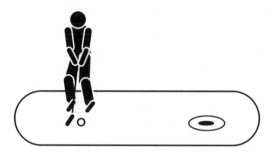

This exercise is presented with a grain of salt. It is recommended for a practice green, but not for the golf course. On the course always aim for a point.

Loosen up your muscles by stretching before you play a round of golf. It is far more important to stretch and relax than it is to go to the driving range and hit balls. The driving range will not get you into the groove, and most golfers hurry too much on the driving range because they do not have enough time. The very act of hurrying will put you into a bad frame of mind. If you would simply go to the first tee and stretch and relax, you will be better prepared.

Putt Three Balls, the Last Two Without Looking

Golfers tend to three-putt more because they have misjudged or mis-hit the distance of a long putt than because they have misread the green. Keep in mind that you should try to contain the distance more than the line when putting long.

Put three or more balls down, four or five inches ahead of each other, as shown.

The main difficulty, and the obstacle which trips most hopefuls before they step up on the first tee, is that they try to remember too many separate bits of instruction.

Oscar Fraley

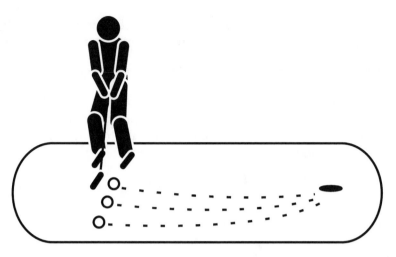

Address the first ball as usual and hit it. Now, without looking up at the line again, putt the rest of the balls. You should already have a reasonably good alignment set up, so if you simply move each foot forward the same amount, your alignment should be well maintained. Repeat this exercise at different points from the hole, different distances and different lines.

Back and Forth

Find a nice, evenly sloped point on a green and mark two spots with tees.

Now putt between these two tees repeatedly. This exercise develops your ability to change the speed of your putting as well as your ability to read slopes. You will notice right away that the ball lines are not the same from one direction to the other; the common misconception that ball lines are segments of circles will be easy to dispel.

Vary the position of the tees and add some slope and some complexity. You will find that this exercise is very good if you have a hard time getting the proper distance on your putts. Feel can be learned through practice. This drill is an excellent example.

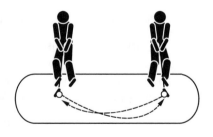

The Rules of Putting 12

This is not an official guide to the rules. It is a loosely worded summary of only those rules that affect the putting game.

Rule 4: Clubs, Balls and Equipment

Rule 4-1: Form and Make of Clubs

A club is an implement for striking the ball.

A putter is a club primarily for use on the putting green.

All clubs are composed of a shaft and a clubhead. There can be no adjustability, which means that all parts are fixed. There are allowances for altering the weight of a club, but the weight cannot be adjustable. It must be fixed onto the club. Lead tape is allowable but you can't add it or take it off during a round.

The shaft should be generally straight. A putter shaft may be joined to the putter head through any point in the head. Gooseneck putter shafts are allowable.

The grip should be substantially straight and should not be molded for any part of the hands. This rule does not include the flat surfaces that are popular on putter grips.

The length of the putter head from heel to toe shall be greater than the breadth from face to back. This precludes circles but not ovals, as long as they are situated correctly.

A putter may have two faces if the loft of each is around the same and neither exceeds 10 degrees. This dual facing sometimes comes in handy when your ball is up against a tree and all you can do is swing left-handed, although these kinds of putters are very uncommon.

A player has addressed the ball only when the club has been grounded. It is a common misconception that address occurs when a player has taken his stance or begun his backswing. In cases where the ball may move, it is best to not ground the club at all, for this will avoid penalties if the ball moves.

The putter face shall have no inward curvature and shall be hard and rigid (in relation to the hardness and rigidity of a ball). Rubber insets are not acceptable. Insets or attachments to the putter face are allowed, so long as they satisfy the other rules.

Rule 4-2: Playing Characteristics Not to be Changed

You cannot purposely change the playing characteristics of a putter during a round of golf.

Any putter which ceases to conform to the above rules during a round due to normal use may not be used for the remainder of the round in its present condition. If you get angry and slam your putter against a tree, then you must return the putter to the satisfaction of the rules prior to using it again. If this is impossible, you cannot use that putter and you cannot substitute another putter which does conform. If your putter breaks accidentally, you may substitute another putter during the round being played.

No foreign material may be put onto the putter face for the purpose of altering its playing characteristics. No oil may be put onto the surface for the purpose of eliminating or reducing friction. Sometimes golfers with bad slices put oil on their clubfaces so as to decrease the slicing. This is clearly taboo.

If your putter conformed to the equipment rules when it was new, then it will always do so as long as the only modifications have been from normal wear and tear. It is unlikely that your putter will experience normal wear and tear that would materially change it characteristics.

Note that you may add lead tape before a round of golf, but not during the round of golf.

Rule 4-4: Maximum of 14 Clubs

No more than 14 clubs may be carried in a bag. Partners may share a putter provided that the total number of clubs used by the partners does not exceed 14. Since this is the number of clubs any individual may carry in his bag, this rule would seem to suggest that you do not want to share a putter with your partner.

Rule 5: The Ball

If you buy standard golf balls, it should be presumed that they are conforming. It is therefore not necessary to get into the specific rules of a golf ball.

The Art and Science of Putting

In general, most golf balls are around 1.68" in diameter. Do not use screwy golf balls, especially those that come with extravagant claims about distance and accuracy. Anything that sounds too good to be true certainly is when it comes to the game of golf.

Rule 5-2: Foreign Materials

Don't add foreign material or alter golf balls in any way. Printing names and logos are allowed, provided the ink does not alter the properties of the ball in a material way. Scuffing and nicking are illegal. Soaking in turpentine is a wives' tale which simply does not work.

Rule 5-3: Ball Unfit for Play

If a ball becomes unfit for play, the player must announce that he is examining the ball, and mark its spot suitably so that another ball may be put into play in that exact spot. Make sure that your opponent or playing partner goes along with your assessment of unplayability, or you may suffer a penalty.

If a ball breaks into pieces as a result of a stroke, the stroke may be replayed without penalty. The possibility of this happening on the green is rather remote.

Rule 7: Practice

Rule 7-1: Prior or Between Rounds

A player may practice putting or chipping on the competition surface prior to starting a round of golf only for match play. No practice is permitted for stroke play prior to a round of golf (on the competitive surface, that is; the practice green is all right).

Rule 7-2: During a Round

A player may practice on the putting green of the last hole that he has played, provided that this practice does not slow down play. Note that it is illegal to practice a full swing (by making contact with a ball, that is), although practicing a short chip is legal. You see the pros do this every once in awhile. Before going on to the next hole, they occasionally practice a couple of times on the green they just finished. It is rare to see someone do this just after they have made a good putt. They usually do it only when they have blown it.

Golf is like solitaire. When you cheat, you cheat only yourself.

Tomy Lema

Rule 8: Advice, Indicating Line of Play

Advice is just what it sounds like. Information, on the other hand, is not advice. Information is such fact as location of a restroom, position of a hazard, etc. Advice concerns how to avoid the hazard or how to approach the rest room. Any indication of what a putt will do on a green is advice, and not information. Giving the amount of break is advice because it is an opinion and is based on conditions; it is not simply a fact.

Rule 8-1: Advice

In general, a player may only give or receive advice from a partner or from a partner's or one's own caddie. In a team situation, the captain may also give advice. On the putting green, the same three individuals (plus a captain) may indicate the target line, but the green shall not be touched in so doing. A flagstick may be held over the target line, but should never touch the green. A caddie or playing partner may stand with his toe on an extension of the target line while he is tending the pin. No mark can be placed to indicate a line under any circumstances.

Under no circumstances can anyone show you a putt for the purpose of illustrating its line to you. This rule seeks to prevent a buddy dropping a ball near yours and hitting it so as to show you the break. And it certainly precludes you from rolling a ball on the green prior to attempting a putt.

Robert Rawson obtained a patent for a putting stroke analyzer that tells you if your putter face is skewed, or if your putter path is skewed. All you have to do is hit it just like you would hit a golf ball. Now here's the problem: Before you hit it, you have to set it up on the putting surface in the exact position that you want to hit the ball. For a 20-foot putt, an error between the target line and the ball line of only one degree will amount to a 4.2 inch error at the hole, which is clearly enough to cause a missed putt. The tolerance of a little mechanical device such as this will be far greater than one degree. Add that to the tolerance of how well you can set it up before you hit it and you have a very inexact science here.

Rule 10: Order of Play

The ball farthest from the hole shall be played first. If two balls are equal from the hole, the decision is made by a draw. Don't get into ridiculous measurement processes here; be reasonable. If you feel as though you need to argue this point with a competitor, maybe the two of you should go into the clubhouse and have a couple of beers and lighten up.

There is no penalty for playing out of turn unless the playing out of turn is done for some competitive advantage.

In general, a golfer has the right to continue putting once he has attempted a stroke, regardless of whether he is now the farthest from the pin or not. Note that this is not the case if you putt from the fringe, for that doesn't count as a putt. If you putt from the fringe to within an inch of the cup, you may not putt out unless you get permission from other golfers already on the putting surface.

Rule 13: Ball Played as it Lies

In general, you may not improve your lie. With regards to putting, this means that you may not move the ball around so as to gain a competitive advantage. You may not move the ball over two inches because you are in a small rut, although you may move your ball if you are obstructed or interfered with.

Rule 13-3: Building a Stance

You cannot build a stance. You cannot stand on anything but the golf course. You cannot kneel on anything but the golf course. You cannot modify the golf course to better your competitive position. You cannot scrape a pile of dirt so that you can stand on it.

Rule 14: Striking the Ball

A stroke is a forward movement of the clubface in order to strike the ball. If you miss the ball you have still made a stroke. Intent is the key; if you try to hit the ball and fail, you have made a stroke. If you jab at a two inch putt and hit the grass and not the ball, you have just made a stroke.

Rule 14-1: Ball to Be Fairly Struck At

The ball should be fairly struck at, not pushed, scraped or spooned. Struck seems to be the key word here. You cannot place the putter face on the back of the ball and then shove it at the

Golf etiquette is kind of like the second verse of the national anthem; good stuff but read by practically nobody.

Herb Graffis

hole. You must strike it, which certainly implies taking a backswing.

Rule 14-2: Assistance or Protection From the Elements

Don't have your partner or your caddie hold an umbrella over your head while you are putting. You may have the umbrella held while you line up, take your stance and get ready, but once you make a stroke, you must be in the elements.

Rule 14-3: Artificial Devices and Unusual Equipment

No artificial devices shall be used. This includes all kinds of practice gear.

Non-artificial items that can be used include throwing a handkerchief to gauge the wind, eyeglasses, and hand warmers.

Illegal: golf ball warmers (although you may certainly put a golf ball into your pocket and use it on the next hole), range finders, putting aid equipment.

Rule 14-4: Striking the Ball More Than Once

If you strike the ball twice in one swing, count two strokes. If you strike the ball three or more times, consider yourself special for having experienced a very rare feat, then count all the times you hit the ball.

Rule 14-5: Playing a Moving Ball

You cannot strike a moving ball. Once you have taken a stance and your ball moves, you are liable for a penalty. If you are unsure whether your ball is about to start rolling, do not take your stance until just before you putt. This may be the case if your ball is resting precariously on a steep incline. If the ball starts to roll before you take a stance, it is simply part of the last stroke played and there is no penalty. Taking a stance is the key.

Rule 15: Wrong Ball

A wrong ball is someone else's ball or a ball other than the one in play (range ball for instance or a ball that has been "found"). If you can't identify your ball without a doubt, you are hitting a wrong ball. If a player has holed out with a wrong ball, he may rectify his mistake before leaving the putting green.

Note that this rule implies that you cannot substitute a new, shiny ball on the putting green unless your old ball has been

Player X has a tap-in putt. When he addresses the ball, it is moved by a gust of wind, right into the cup. The ball must be replaced and a penalty of one stroke is added to the score. (Rule 18-2b)

The Art and Science of Putting

damaged. You cannot use a water ball to tee off, and then use a new ball on the green.

Rule 16: The Putting Green

The putting green is all ground around the hole being played which is specially prepared for putting or otherwise defined as such. A ball is on the green when any part of it touches the green. A ball resting against the fringe is on the green. If in doubt, the ball is on the green.

There are still some golf courses that use smoothed sand in place of grass. This is then the putting green for these courses.

Rule 16-1: General Putting Rules

A line of putt may never be touched except to move loose soil or other impediments from the line by picking them up by hand or brushing them aside with a putter. Note that you may not use any other implements to move the ball. You cannot use your hat or a towel, for instance.

In addressing the ball, a player may place the club in front of the ball without pressing down. Some pros seem to like to do this in order to get their line. It is difficult to see what this may do, but personal preference is important and the rules allow it.

In lifting the ball and in measuring, the line may be touched.

If an old hole or ball mark obstructs the line, these may be repaired.

If a moveable obstacle is in the way, it may be moved. Moveable obstacles are not a part of the golf course.

It should also be noted that moving standing water is a no-no. As will be seen later, relief is possible from standing water, but it may not be moved or fixed in any way.

Lifted Ball

A ball on the putting green may be lifted and cleaned and then placed back in the same spot.

Testing the Surface

You may never test the surface by rolling a ball or roughening or scraping. This means you cannot scrape the back of your putter across the surface to see how the grain lies (contrary to what some books may say!). You may not pick up your ball and then roll it over to the side of the green where your bag sits.

A club may have a design that allows for an adjustment in the weight of the club. The adjustment must not be made during a round of golf.

The Rules of Putting

125

Standing on the Line of the Putt

You may not stand on the line of the putt, nor with one foot on each side of the line (croquet style). Your caddie or partner or his caddie may not stand on the line of the putt, or beyond the hole on the line of the putt (extension to the line of the putt).

Other Ball in Motion

Don't hit your ball while any other ball is in motion on the green.

Ball Overhanging Hole

If you take a putt and the ball stops, overhanging the hole, you have a reasonable amount of time to get to the ball, and then another ten seconds to determine if the ball is at rest. If by then the ball is still overhanging the hole, you will need to hit it in (and don't jab at it because if you miss it, you have taken another stroke). If you just stand there staring for more than the allotted time, you get a penalty. And of course, no blowing on the ball or banging on the green surface just behind the ball.

Rule 16-2: Conceding Opponent's Next Stroke: Match Play

You can always concede your opponents next shot as long as his ball is not moving. The opponent, of course, counts the conceded stroke but then the ball is considered as holed out.

Rule 17: The Flagstick

The flagstick may be attended only on authority of the player before he plays his stroke. If the flagstick is not attended before the ball is in play, it cannot be attended or removed while the ball is in motion.

A flagstick must be attended during putting. It should either be removed before striking the ball or removed after striking the ball. Note that it is not a penalty if the flagstick is not removed and the ball does not hit it.

Rule 17-3: Ball Striking Flagstick or Attendant

You must attend and remove a flagstick when striking a ball from the putting surface. When you are off the putting surface, you have a choice of what to do, but you must declare your choice

Players X and Y are partners. Player X hits from off the green, at which point Player Y runs over to the pin and removes it just as the ball falls into the hole. Since Rule 17-1 states that the flagstick must be attended before the shot is played, they lose the hole.

The Art and Science of Putting

Charles Bertas obtained a patent for an optical device for reading golf greens. This is really very simple, although illegal on a golf course. It would be pretty easy to make something like this for yourself, and it would probably be a good idea, as long as it was made the right way. The problem with plumb bobbing is that the putter gives you a vertical reference, not a horizontal one. You could duplicate this invention by simply taping a perpendicular corner to your putter (some stiff cardboard will do nicely). Don't worry about patent infringement; the patent expired a long time ago, so it is now public property.

before striking the ball. If the ball strikes the flagstick or an attendant, you are liable for a penalty.

Rule 17-4: Ball Resting Against Flagstick

If your ball is resting against the flagstick when the flagstick is in the hole, the player or someone authorized by him may move or remove the flagstick. If the ball falls into the hole, the player shall be deemed to have holed out at his last stroke. Otherwise, the ball, if moved, shall be placed on the lip of the hole, without penalty. It would seem obvious that one should never have to place the ball onto the lip of the hole unless one is very careless in removing, or moving the flagstick. By simply wiggling it, which is well within the rules, the ball should fall down into the hole.

Rule 18: Ball at Rest Moved

A ball is deemed to have moved if it leaves its position and comes to rest in any other place.

Rule 18-1: By Outside Agency

If a ball at rest is moved by an outside agency, the player shall incur no penalty and the ball shall be replaced before the player plays another stroke. If the ball moved is not recoverable, another ball may be substituted.

In general, if your ball is moved in any way by an outside agency, try to locate the spot it was in before it was moved, and

There is no provision in the rules of golf which specifies a minimum distance that a hole may be placed from the edge of the green. Practical constraints and the enjoyment of a practical layout dictate a minimum of around three feet, but two inches is legal.

The Rules of Putting

replace it at that point. By the way, it must be replaced; it used to be an option, but no longer.

If your ball is hit by another ball, try to replace your ball into its original location as best you can. The ball that hit your ball, incidentally, must be played from where it eventually comes to rest. This occasionally creates some interesting situations.

You must also mark your ball when picking it up to examine or clean on the putting surface. Failure to do so will result in a penalty.

Rule 19: Ball in Motion Deflected or Stopped

Rule 19-1: By Outside Agency

If a ball in motion is accidentally deflected or stopped by any outside agency, it is a rub of the green (rub of the green is a kind way of saying, "Too bad for you"). No penalty is incurred and the ball should be played as it lies. If the moving ball is deflected or stopped by, or comes to rest in or on any moving or animate outside agency, the stroke shall be canceled and the ball shall be replaced. This is, of course, providing that you do not do the deflection or stopping yourself. If the ball is not recoverable, replace it.

Rule 19-2: By Player, Partner or Caddie or Equipment

If any of the above parties stops the ball, in match play the player loses the hole, in stroke play a penalty is incurred and the ball is played as it lies.

If a ball comes to rest on your competitor's clothing or equipment, it should be dropped as near as possible to where the article was when the ball came to rest in or on it.

Rule 19-3: Stopped by Competitor in Match Play

If a competitor deliberately stops your ball, he loses the hole in match play. If it is done accidentally, no penalty is incurred and you may elect to play the ball as it lies, or replay the shot without penalty.

Rule 19-4: Stopped by Competitor, Caddie or Equipment in Stroke Play

This is a case of Rule 19-1; Outside Agency.

During the 1977 TPC, JC Snead's panama hat blew off his head and travelled straight down the fairway and struck his ball. A penalty of two strokes.

The Art and Science of Putting

Rule 19-5: By a Ball At Rest

If your ball hits a ball at rest, the ball at rest is replaced as best as possible and you must play your ball as it lies. This would certainly seem to give good reason to have any ball that might be in your way marked so that your ball does not hit it. In stroke play, when a ball at rest is deflected by another ball which has been struck on the putting green, that player with the resting ball suffers a two stroke penalty. So if you hit a resting ball when you are on the putting surface, both parties suffer penalties. Mark your ball when in doubt. Both parties suffer when balls collide on the putting green (unless one of the balls came from off the surface).

It is interesting that the original rules of golf forbid marking of balls on the green. It was common tactic to actually play your ball so that it would be in the way of a competitor's (called a stymie). You can see how the game is made better by the new rules, since the goal should be to obtain a low score, not stymie your competitor. With the new rules, you have only yourself to blame for your score.

Rule 20: Relief Situations

In general, a ball is "placed" on the green (as opposed to dropped) when relief situations are encountered. The ball should be marked with a small marker directly behind the ball. If the marker interferes with another player's line of play, the marker should be moved to one side or the other, usually by placing the putter head next to the ball and placing the marker at the toe of the putter. This process may be repeated several times until the marker is free of the other players putting line.

Rule 20-3: Placing and Replacing

If it is impossible to determine the spot where the ball is to be placed, the ball shall be placed as near as possible to the place where it lay but not nearer the hole.

Joseph Rango obtained a patent for a golf putter with a hole through the center of the head. The hole does two things. First, it may be used gauge how round the ball is. Second, it increases the breadth of the sweet spot by increasing the moment of inertia (which might be very helpful).

In July of 1964, Bill Carey was playing a match at the Roehampton Golf Course in England. It was very near dusk when the two players teed off, and when they got to the hole, Bill could not find his ball so after a while he conceded the hole. He then found his ball in the cup, thereby losing the hole after shooting a hole in one.

If the ball fails to remain on the spot it is placed, it shall be replaced without penalty. If it still fails to remain on that spot, it shall be placed at the nearest spot not nearer the hole where it can be placed at rest.

Rule 20-5: Playing Next Stroke from Previous Stroke Site

When, under the Rules, a player elects or is required to play his next stroke from where a previous stroke was played, he shall place his ball at that spot of the previous stroke as best he can.

Rule 21: Cleaning Ball

A ball may always be picked up and cleaned while on the putting surface. A ball may not be substituted in this situation unless the original ball is deemed unplayable.

You cannot lift and clean your ball when it lies off the putting green, regardless of whether you intend to putt from that point. If your ball is obstructing another player's ball and you must lift it and mark it, you may not clean it if it is not on the green.

Rule 22: Ball Interfering with or Assisting Play

If your ball might assist any other player or interfere any other player you must lift it and mark it. When in doubt, lift and mark.

Rule 23: Loose Impediments

Stones, leaves, twigs, bugs, dead birds, branches and things that aren't fixtures of the golf course are considered loose impediments. On the putting green, sand and loose soil are also impediments. Snow and ice are either casual water or loose impediments, at the option of the player. Dew is never considered a loose impediment.

Rule 23-1: Relief

A loose impediment may be removed, provided a player's ball is not in motion. When a ball is in motion, nothing may be moved. A twig or branch in a hazard may not be moved, but a cigarette butt may be moved wherever it lies; it is an obstruction, not a loose impediment.

Rule 24: Obstructions

An obstruction is anything artificial. This word should be self-explanatory. Roads, walls, fences, immovable objects which

Player X gets livid over three putting from two feet and throws his putter into a pond. He then sends his caddie back to the clubhouse for another putter. He has broken the rules of golf and must suffer a two stroke per hole penalty, not to exceed four strokes.

The Art and Science of Putting

are out of bounds are obstructions. Soda cans, cigarette butts, turkey sandwiches are also obstructions.

As long as the ball does not lie in or on the obstruction, the obstruction may be removed. If the ball moves, there is no penalty.

When a ball is in motion, no obstructions may be moved except the flagstick and equipment.

Rule 24-2: Immovable Obstruction Interference

If an obstruction interferes with a player's stance or line or putt, the player may move the ball and place it in the nearest position which affords relief from the interference, but not nearer the hole. If the ball rolls back into the condition, replace until satisfactory resolution.

You do not have to stand on a sprinkler head if you are on the putting surface. However, if a sprinkler head is in your line of putt when you are off the green, but you are not standing on it, you may not get relief. You will presumably have to chip over the obstruction in this case. Too bad, but that's the way it is.

Rule 25: Abnormal Conditions

Casual water is any temporary accumulation of water on the course which is visible before or after the player takes his stance and is not in a water hazard. Snow and ice are either casual water or loose impediments, at the option of the player.

Ground under repair is any portion of the course so marked by order of the Committee, or so declared by its authorized representative. It includes material piled for removal and a hole made by a greenskeeper, even if not so marked. Stakes and lines defining ground under repair are also ground under repair. Stakes may also be obstructions from which relief may be secured.

Old grass which has been left to rot is not ground under repair.

Rule 25-1: Casual Water, Ground Under Repair and Damage

When a ball touches ground under repair, a hole, or a runway made by a burrowing animal, reptile or bird, it is considered interference and appropriate relief may be secured. On the green, interference also occurs if these conditions affect the player's line of putt.

Player X does not have a coin in his pocket to mark his ball. Instead, he uses a driver, placing the driver down on the green with the end of the shaft at the point of the ball. He picks up his ball and cleans it and then replaces his ball. This is legal, since the rules of golf do not specify ball markers.

The Rules of Putting

This means that if there is a puddle on the green that is in your putting line, you are entitled to relief. Lift the ball and place it in the spot nearest the original lie, no nearer to the hole or in a hazard.

Note that if your ball is just off the green, you may not move it to avoid standing water in your line. The ball must be on the green to enjoy this rule.

Local Rules

Many golf courses adopt local rules. These are usually posted at the starter's desk. Such things as winter rules, extreme wetness and other forms of relief are included. These generally affect the play through the green more than the putting surface, but there are sometimes conditions which merit special relief on the putting surface, particularly conditions of standing water or parched ground.

Parched ground on a putting surface is sometimes condition for relief. Fertilizer may be spread too liberally causing the grass to die. Or a drought might be causing occasional brown spots to interfere with effective play.

When local rules allow, relief may be secured from these conditions, much like relief from standing water.

Etiquette

While etiquette falls into the category of common courtesy, the following items should be treated as rules for all practical purposes. It is far more annoying to your playing partners if you breach etiquette than if you break a rule (unless you are betting).

1) Do not walk over somebody's line, for you may press down and leave an imprint. This rule is meticulously followed by the pros.

The recommended length of a flagstick is seven feet. This is a recommendation only. There are some mechanisms on the market that measure the distance from a pin by use of the flagstick height. Since the height may vary, these devices are inadvisable.

The Art and Science of Putting

2) Stand to the side when someone is putting. You may stand behind, but this is sometimes very annoying.

3) Do not move around when somebody is putting. This is distracting.

4) Do not cast shadows onto somebody's line while they are putting. Do not stand with the flagstick next to the hole and cast a shadow on the hole; this is the worst thing you can do.

5) Although the rules generally specify the farthest ball from the hole to be putt first, sometimes it is more practical for a ball very close to the hole to be putt out first. The ball closest should ask prior to putting out.

6) When you walk up to a putting green, always leave your golf bag on the side of the green closest to the next tee area. That way you will not have to go over when the hole is finished, get your bag and walk around, thereby forcing the golfers behind you to wait.

7) Never stand on a green and mark your scorecard after holing out. Get off the green, over to the next tee area first.

8) Do not set your bag down on a green.

The Real Rules

Most everybody cheats at golf in some way or another. At the very least, we all kick our ball out of the rough once in awhile, and even if we are not keeping score, that constitutes cheating. Here are some excellent cheating methods that should be used with discretion.

Extension #1) The Law of Physics Prevails

The laws of physics take precedence over the rules of golf, at all times. If any action occurs which violates a law of physics, that shot may be taken over again, or a suitable correction to the end result may be applied so as to rectify the violation.

For instance, if your ball is putt directly at the hole, but it jumps over the hole, that violates the law of gravity and the ball shall be deemed to have gone into the hole.

If your ball is heading directly at the hole, but at the last instant it jumps to the side and slides past the hole, that violates the law of inertia and it shall be deemed to have gone into the hole.

Mary Brown was playing in the Southern California Women's Open when play was halted due to rain. Upon returning to play, Mary putted her ball, which promptly slid over the hole because the hole had filled up with water. Tournament officials allowed her to re-hit her putt, declaring that she had been unfairly victimized.

If a slope on a green is such that any putt struck from above the hole simply rolls off the green, regardless of how lightly that ball was struck, the ball shall be deemed to have gone into the hole.

Extension #2) Neutrality of Weather

If your ball comes to rest on the lip of the hole, and you wait the maximum amount of time and it still has not gone into the hole, you may blow on it, for on a different day, in different weather, there may have been a wind blowing on that exact hole, in that very direction, and that wind would have caused the ball to go into the hole.

The same may be said of any putt which comes close to the hole, for on a different day, in different weather conditions, the ball would have gone into the hole with a slight difference in weather pattern.

Extension #3) Elimination of Chance

If a ball strikes a flagstick, it shall be deemed to have gone into the hole, for the game of golf should never be subject to the vagaries of chance. If it could be argued that 10 equally hit balls might have resulted in five going into the hole, and five bouncing away, then all 10 shall be deemed to have gone into the hole.

Another interpretation of this rule suggests that you may replay a ball which rolls awkwardly or crookedly. A golf green should be flat and smooth and should never contain pits or burrows which distort the trajectory. This is not the problem of the golfer, but sloppiness and laziness on the part of the greenskeepers who are probably in the maintenance building drinking beer and watching television when they should be out perfecting the greens.

Likewise, a ball which rolls over a twig or a chunk of hail or any other randomly deposited debris from mother nature may be hit again from its original location, after that debris has been removed and suitably discarded.

Extension #4) Impossible Shot

No shot in golf shall be deemed impossible. If your ball lies such that a sand trap is directly between your ball and the pin, you may move your ball so that the putt can be made. No golf

Player X is marking his ball and his hand accidentally slips and knocks the ball. There is no penalty and the ball may be replaced to its original spot.

The Art and Science of Putting

course should be designed so that impossible shots are encountered.

This rule is particularly useful on multiple tiered greens, since everyone knows that putting on these ridiculous contrivances is impossible on the face of it. You may move your ball onto the tier that presently contains the pin.

This rule is also useful on those ridiculous kidney shaped greens. It should never be the case that a straight line putt must travel over anything but nice, smooth green.

Extension #5) Avoidance of Embarrassment

The founding fathers of the game never intended the game to be humiliating. If a putt is so short that a player will subject himself to embarrassment if he should try to make it and miss, that putt shall be picked up and deemed holed out on the next shot. Of course this rule may be interpreted differently by different handicap players.

This rule may also be interpreted to say that no player shall ever have to hit a fourth putt, since hitting four putts is very embarrassing (unless, of course, if the net result of the first three putts has left the ball somewhere off the green, in which case the player must pick up his ball and quit the game of golf).

Extension #6) Academy Award Performance

Any player that misses a putt, regardless of how far his ball comes to rest from the hole, and then subsequently picks his ball up with such a convincing grimace and gesticulation of arms and hands that it is obvious to everyone that he would never in a million, billion, zillion, killion years miss the next putt, that next putt shall be deemed a gimme.

The same rule applies to the short putt "stabber" who is clearly bored with and annoyed with the prospect of having to hit such a short, stupid, easy putt. If the result of the stab is a miss, the stab shall be deemed as made nevertheless simply as a way of rectifying the absurdity of the situation.

Extension #7) Mutually Negotiated Concession of Putts

Any plurality of players may, at any time, concede putts to each other. For instance, Player A may have a very difficult 30-foot putt, Player B may have an easier 20-foot putt, and player C may lie off the green in a hazard. By mutual consent, the

In 1921, P.M. Gregor hit a long putt which came to rest on the lip of the hole. A grasshopper then landed on the ball, thereby giving it a slight push needed to sink the putt.

three players may all pick up their balls and record a score as though their next shots were holed out.

Extension #8) Angry Forgetfulness

Any player who gets so angry that he stops counting his strokes shall record a bogey for that hole. The game of golf was never intended to be maddening.

Extension #9) Cue Stick

A putter may be used like a pool cue stick at any time, provided the player does not wear white pants. However, once the putter is used as a cue stick, it must be used as a cue stick for the rest of the round. (In keeping with the overall attempt of this book to be an instructional guide, it should be mentioned that it is very important to follow through when using the putter as a cue-stick. Most beginners tend to poke at the ball, failing their follow through, which results in a ball short of the hole. Also keep in mind that you need to impart forward English to the ball, so try to hit it just above center. You might consider bringing a chunk of cue stick chalk with you, but not if you are wearing white pants.)

Extension #10) Hand Wedge

A player may throw his ball once during any round of golf. This extension is closely related to the Mulligan, but applies on the green as well.

Extension #11) Twilight Conditions

If it is too dark to see the hole, it is well past time to pick up your ball and go home to your wife (or husband or dog or television).

Extension #12) Ball Marking

When marking your ball, you may place the coin as close to the hole as you can get away with. When replacing your ball you may place it as close to the hole as you can get away with. This means that you can multiply by two the distance that you can get away with. As a side point, it is a common courtesy of golf to look the other way when a member of your foursome is marking or replacing their ball.

Player X is playing golf at a rather unkempt golf course. His ball lies on the green, but running water is pushing on the ball. Just as he makes his swing, the ball moves a little bit and he strikes it. This is legal since the rules allow for a ball to be played from running water.

The Art and Science of Putting

Extension #13) Innocently Rolling Ball on Line

A player may innocently roll a ball over his line by first placing his bag at the edge of the green opposite the hole from where his ball lies.

He may then pretend to be simply rolling his ball toward his bag so as to be able to clean it with the towel (must have a towel on bag to qualify for this extension). The player must also pretend to be looking in another direction, not watching how the ball rolls, and finally, he must then actually go over to his bag and clean the ball. The player must take great pains to appear innocent in every respect.

Extension #14) Plausible Deniability

A player may break any rule of golf provided he has an excellent reason for so doing. Simple ignorance is not an allowable reason. Personal safety is always a good reason. It should be noted that attorneys gain quite a scoring advantage from this rule, for they are exceptional practitioners of absurd, but reluctantly acceptable arguments.

Extension #15) Weenie Rule (Let it Be)

Any player may, at any time, challenge another player for a rule violation. If the challenging player does not have in his procession a current rulebook of golf which unequivocally articulates said rule, that challenging player shall be disqualified for being a weenie. If that player actually has a rulebook, he shall be disqualified for being a weenie. The founding fathers never intended the game to be played by weenies.

In the 1925 US Open, Bobby Jones' ball moved as he addressed it. He called the penalty on himself, despite the fact that nobody else had seen the movement. The penalty cost him the championship. When asked, he said, "There's only one way to play the game. You might as well praise a man for not robbing a bank as to praise him for playing by the rules."

Glossary of Putting Terminology

Albatross — A score of three under par for a single hole.

Barber — A player who talks too much and distracts other players.

Bent Grass — A finely textured type of grass especially common in cooler climates.

Bermuda Grass — A coarse, rubbery feeling grass with intertwined blades especially common in hot climates.

Blade Putter — The shaft meets one end of the clubface.

Break — The amount of slope determines the break of a putt. In general, break is referred to as the distance from the hole that the target line passes, i.e., nine inches of break.

Center Shafted Putter — The shaft meets toward the center of the clubface. This places the sweet spot close to the center of balance.

Charge — A philosophical term used to describe an aggressive attitude toward reaching the hole. The charging golfer rarely leaves a putt short. Arnold Palmer is the most famous example.

Claw Grip — A grip used with the long shafted putters wherein the index and middle fingers resemble a bird's foot structure.

It's good sportsmanship to not pick up lost golf balls while they're still rolling.

Mark Twain

Cross-Handed Grip — The upper and lower hands switch positions from the normal golf grip.

Flange Blade Putter — A straight bladed putter with a mass added to the back of the putter head.

Foozle — A bad shot which may also be called a dub or a duff.

Forged Head — A putter head which is made by pounding or slamming a piece of metal into the desired shape. Blacksmiths forge metal by heating it and then hammering it into the shape they want. Modern manufacturing techniques are considerably more advanced, but the idea is the same.

Fringe — The collar around a green which is usually mowed to a level intermediate between the green level and the fairway level. The fringe is not a part of the green.

Frog Hair — The short grass around the green. Nickname for fringe.

Gimmee — A putt which does not have to be holed out, but which counts as a stroke for the hole total.

Gobble — A putt that unexpectedly lands in the hole.

Gooseneck — A flange that extends outward and forward from the putter head. Goosenecks are often investment casted as part of the clubhead proper.

Hosel — The socket into which the shaft of a club is fitted. Many putters do not have a hosel, as the shaft is extended outward and upward from the putter clubface as one piece (like a gooseneck).

In the Grip — A putt closer to the hole than the distance of a putter's grip. It is often the case that any putt within the grip is a gimmee (which of course violates the rules of golf but may be considered good etiquette and good sportsmanship).

During the 1950 US Open, Lloyd Mangrum picked up his ball to remove a gnat which had landed on it just prior to Lloyd's stroke. He failed to mark the ball first, however, and was penalized two strokes. He eventually tied Ben Hogan and then lost the playoff.

In the Leather — A putt closer to the hole than the distance between a putter's head and its grip. This is a more liberal interpretation than "in the grip."

Investment Casting — A manufacturing process wherein the clubhead is made of a one piece molded metal mass. This is a very common technique.

Lag — To hit a long putt so as to ensure that it will stop near the hole. This is in contrast to actually attempting to make a putt.

Mallet-head Putter — The shaft joins near the end of the clubface at a steep angle, and the head is heavy and shaped like a half moon. Mallets require a very upright swing, thereby forcing the eyes over the target line.

Neutral Grip — Neither hand dominates the other, and the grip is neither too tight nor too soft.

Overlapping Grip — The little finger of the bottom hand interlocks with the index finger of the top hand.

Plumb Bobbing — The process of holding a putter in front while viewing a potential putt so as to be able to read the slope of the putt.

Pop Putter — A golfer who putts with very active hands, as opposed to shoulders and arms.

Reverse Overlap Grip — The index finger of the upper hand overlaps one or more knuckles of the lower hand.

Rub of the Green — Tough Luck! When a ball in motion is stopped or deflected by an outside agency. The ball is left to lie where it ends up, even if that means it is knocked off the green or into a sewer pipe.

Skulling — Hitting a chip or pitch shot too hard and sending the ball past the green.

Sole — To hold a golf club so that the entire bottom of the head touches the grass. This means that the lie is equal to the angle of the shaft. Soling a putter is not necessary, and is probably not done very often, strictly speaking.

During the 1940 US Open, Lawson Little hit his ball onto the green where it was then picked up and carried away by a Persian cat. Little was allowed to respot the ball. There was no word on what the cat might have done with the golf ball.

Glossary of Putting Terminology

141

Stony — A shot where the ball lands close to the flagstick.

Straight-blade Putter — A thin, lightweight head useful for fast putts.

Stroke Putter — A golfer who putts with passive hands, meaning the activity is generated by the arms or the shoulders. This is opposed to a Pop Putter.

Stymie — Long ago, this term referred to the situation where an opponent's ball blocked your ball. The rules have been changed to allow marking, so now the term has ancillary meanings. Stymie used to be part of the strategy of golf, much like playing eight ball on a billiard table wherein you block the entrance to a hole with your own ball so that your opponent cannot sink his ball into that hole.

Taking the Pipe — Choking, folding, blowing it, losing your cool.

Texas Wedge — A putter used to play from a sand trap. This term comes from the fact that hot summers in Texas often dry out the sand so much that it is easier and safer to putt the ball over the hard surface than to blast or chip.

Whiff — A complete miss. This is not uncommon on the putting green where players often stab at a one inch putt and then end up missing it completely. It also counts as a stroke in the rules of golf. And it is probably one of the most ignored rules of all.

Yips — A common affliction on short putts, characterized by inexplicable jerks and twitches. This is a psychological problem, not a physical one.

In the 1960 Texas Open, Paul Farmer decided to change putters after the front nine. After completing the round he learned he had been fined two strokes per hole for the entire back nine for a total of eighteen penalty strokes (rule has since changed to four strokes maximum).

The Art and Science of Putting

About the Author

Rik DeGunther graduated cum laude from University of Illinois with a degree in Engineering Physics in 1979, and subsequently obtained an MS from Stanford University in 1982. He has enjoyed a career in high-tech design and management since 1979, mostly in the San Francisco Bay Area and Sacramento, California.

Rik has played golf most of his life, achieving a low handicap along the way. He has been analyzing the technical and emotional aspects of putting for the last ten years, of which efforts this book is a result.

Golf is a good walk spoiled.
Mark Twain

Sink a Hole-In-One with Masters Press!

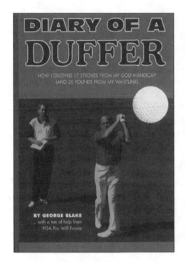

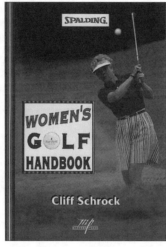

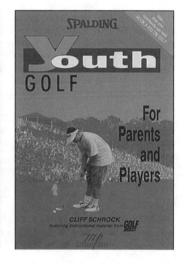

Diary of a Duffer
George Blake

This book is a humorous look at one man's quest for better golfing. You'll laugh as you pick up tips that helped one duffer cut his woeful 34 handicap in half.

$12.95 • ISBN 1-57028-020-7

Women's Golf Handbook
Cliff Schrock

An intelligent explanation of the sport with attention paid to the special needs of female players.

$12.95 • ISBN 1-57028-032-0

Youth Golf
Cliff Schrock

Will help coaches and players make the most of their practice time. Includes information from the National Youth Sports Coaches Association on how to develop youth league golf leagues.

$12.95 • ISBN 0-940279-87-8

Masters Press has a complete line of books that cover golf and other sports to help coaches and participants alike "master their game." All of our books are available at better bookstores or by calling Masters Press at 1-800-9-SPORTS. Catalogs available by request.